MAPLE SUGAR

★

FROM SAP TO SYRUP

THE HISTORY, LORE, AND HOW-TO

BEHIND THIS SWEET TREAT

★

TIM HERD

Storey Publishing

TO WALT JONES AND BOB SHAY,

who hired me as a green (read: totally inexperienced) naturalist; trained me in natural history and environmental education; encouraged me in my professional career; and for many years have proven invaluable as mentors, colleagues, and friends.

The mission of Storey Publishing is to serve our customers by publishing practical information that encourages personal independence in harmony with the environment.

Edited by Lisa H. Hiley and Deborah Burns
Art direction and book design by Alethea Morrison

Front cover photography by © Colin Ericson/ StockFood Munich (bottom left), © Paul Poplis Photography, Inc/StockFood (bottom right and inside front flap)
Back cover photography by © GAP Photos/Julie Dansereau (middle), © Stéphane Groleau/ Alamy (bottom right), © Lonely Planet Images/Alamy (bottom left), © Vespasian/ Alamy (top)

Inside cover photography by © Plainpicture/ Glasshouse Images (front and back)
Interior photography credits appear on page 144
Illustrations by © Beverly Duncan

Indexed by Nancy D. Wood

© 2010 by Tim Herd

Thanks to South Face Farm, Ashfield, Massachusetts, for sharing their maple ephemera collection.

Storey Publishing
210 MASS MoCA Way
North Adams, MA 01247
www.storey.com

Printed in China by Toppan Leefung Printing Ltd.
10 9 8 7 6 5 4 3 2

LIBRARY OF CONGRESS
CATALOGING-IN-PUBLICATION DATA

Herd, Tim.
  Maple sugar / by Tim Herd.
    p. cm.
  Includes index.
  ISBN 978-1-60342-735-7 (pbk. : alk. paper)
  1. Maple sugar. I. Title.
TP395.H47 2011
641.3'364—dc22

2010043059

CONTENTS

MAPLE SPIRIT

IN NORTHEASTERN NORTH AMERICA THRIVES A TREE UNRIVALED in beauty, form, and function. Its stout trunk and graceful branches produce fine, close-grained wood that is perfect for tools, furniture, and firewood. Its spreading crown, thickly draped in hand-shaped leaves, offers a vivid palette of changing colors to the sky and a sheltering security to numerous woodland creatures. And from its very depth issues a sweet sap that forms the sole ingredient of one of the world's most appealing natural delicacies.

Which tree is this, you may be asking? Why, the magnificent maple! The choice sweetness of a maple is revealed in the intricate relationship of the tree's living systems. This is a sliver of its mystery: that an awesomely complex living network of woody beings and basic elements, swirling in the eternal cycle of growth and stasis, offers up such a tasty and tangible product of its majestic spirit.

I invite you to discover more of the remarkable qualities and special gifts of this family of trees. Follow the footsteps of both bygone and present sugarers — and discover the easy step-by-step process — as you learn the lore, tap the trees, secure the sap, separate the sugar, and taste the treat. This is one book with which you can truly enjoy the fruits of your labor. Now that's a sweet deal!

DRAWN FROM WOOD

HOW MAPLE SUGAR CAME TO BE
AN ABNAKI LEGEND

In the early days of the world, life was much easier for man. Gluskap, the Creator, saw to it that the lives of his People were very good, with plenty of food to hunt, gather, and grow. Even the maple tree flowed year-round with sap as sweet and thick as honey.

In those days, Gluskap traveled from village to village to keep an eye on the People. One day he discovered an abandoned village. The houses were in disrepair, the fields were overgrown, the cooking fires had gone cold; he could find no one gathering food, no one preparing to hunt, no dogs barking, and no children playing.

He wondered and wandered about until he heard a strange sound coming from the forest. As he approached, he could tell that it was the sound of many people moaning. But the moaning he heard was not from pain — it was from pleasure! He searched until he found the people of the village in a large stand of beautiful maples, lying at the bases of the trees, and letting the sweet syrup drip into their open mouths.

The maple syrup had fattened them up so much and made them so lazy that they could do nothing but lie about in the grove. Gluskap scolded them to get up, return to their village, rekindle their fires, and tend to their gardens. But the People did not listen. They were content and refused to move.

Highly disturbed by their inactivity, he flew to the lake, filled a bark container with water, returned to the woods, and poured it over the trees to dilute the syrup. Some say he did this thirty times, as many as the days between moons. After a while the People complained that the sap was no longer thick and sweet.

"Now, get up!" Gluskap cried, "and live and work! Because of your laziness, the trees will no longer flow with sweet syrup, but mere sap. If you want the syrup, you must work for it by boiling the sap. And what's more, it will soon vanish. So that you will remember the error of your ways, you will be able to make syrup just once a year and only for a short time!"

He showed them that making the syrup would take much work. In order to re-create the sweetness they so fondly remembered, they would need to make many birch bark containers to collect the sap; gather wood for fires; tend the fires and heat rocks; and constantly add hot rocks to the sap to boil away the water over many days.

And so it is to this day, as the People remember the Creator's lesson and work hard to make the maple syrup they love so much! — ADAPTED FROM WWW.FIRSTPEOPLE.US

ver thousands of years, legendary tales of the maple and its gifts have been reverently recounted by Native Americans, who attribute its primal purity to the Creator. Despite not possessing a written language, nearly all the Eastern Woodland Indian tribes have a similar version of this story in their oral histories.

For example, a comparable story tells of the Earth Mother, Kokomis, who made maple syrup so that it poured out of the trees. Her grandson, Manabush, however, worried that men would become lazy if the sweet gift was so easily obtained, so he climbed to the top of the maple and showered it with water, diluting the syrup to sap.

The Ottowas ascribe the primeval account to their god, Nanahboozhoo, who cast a spell on the sugar maple, turning its pure syrup into sap, for fear his people would become apathetic and weak if Nature's gifts were gained too freely.

It seems that all the tribes realized that while the sweet spirit of the trees is freely offered, there's work involved in order to enjoy it.

Undoubtedly, the native people were skilled observers who made good use of their natural environment; from its abundantly diverse resources they found all they needed to survive and thrive. Fashioning tools from stone, they became accomplished woodworkers; adapting animal techniques for stalking and camouflage, they became expert hunters.

They discovered herbs and developed uses for flavorings, medicines, and poultices; they cultivated crops and knew the cycles of the seasons. Perhaps they noted and imitated the red squirrels nibbling on maple twigs or icicles of frozen sap.

Native people were the first to discover *sinzibuckwud,* the Algonquin word for maple syrup, meaning literally "drawn from wood."

FROM THE IROQUOIS

In another story about the natural bounty of the maple, the Iroquois speak of their ancestor Chief Woksis, who had once lodged his tomahawk deeply into a living tree trunk and left it there overnight. The following day, his wife, Moqua, while absorbed in her quillwork, inadvertently let her cooking pot of meat boil dry. Saving herself a trip to the river for fresh water, she substituted the watery tree sap that had run down the handle of the tomahawk and dripped into a bowl at the base of the wounded tree. Both were amazed at the sweetness of the meat, and the news of the discovery of the maple's hidden bounty spread far and wide.

NATIVE HISTORICAL PERIODS

Archeologists and anthropologists refer to the following terms and periods when describing the cultural histories of the Amerindians (a.k.a. Native Americans or American Indians). Whether sugar making has been practiced throughout all these time frames is not known with any certainty, but historical scientists and modern Native Americans agree that it has been for thousands of years.

PALEO-INDIAN	10,000 TO 8000 BCE
ARCHAIC	8000 TO 1000 BCE
TRANSITIONAL	1800 TO 800 BCE
EARLY WOODLAND	1000 TO 500 BCE
MIDDLE WOODLAND	500 BCE TO 1000 CE
LATE WOODLAND	1000 TO 1550
HISTORIC INDIAN	1550 TO 1760
COLONIAL	1640 TO 1783
EARLY AMERICAN	1783 TO 1850

Indian Legend

An Indian squaw, forgetting her boiling sweet water from the maple tree, found maple sugar in the bottom of her cooking pot, thus pleasing her mighty hunter upon his return.

So was the first maple product eagerly devoured.

EARLY METHOD OF BOILING SYRUP

TABLE SIZE
SKOOKUM
(INDIAN FOR BULLY)
SYRUP
OF PURE CANE AND
MAPLE SUGAR

❧

"There is in some parts of New England a kind of tree whose juice that weeps out of its incision, if it is permitted slowly to exhale away the superfluous moisture, doth congeal into a sweet and saccharin substance and the like was confirmed to me by the agent of the great and populous colony of Massachusetts."

ENGLISH CHEMIST ROBERT BOYLE, *PHILOSOPHICAL WORKS*, 1663

1 POUND NET WEIGHT
SCULLY'S
SKOOKUM
"INDIAN FOR BULLY"
BRAND

PURE
CANE SUGAR
AND
MAPLE SUGAR
SYRUP
PACKED ONLY BY
D. B. Scully Syrup Co.
Chicago.

COPYRIGHT 1925 BY D. B. SCULLY SYRUP CO.

COLLECTING THE SAP

In preparation for the maple sugaring season, the Woodland tribes made sap containers of birch bark called *mokuks*, which were sewn together with strips of elm bark and sealed with pine resin. Each mokuk could hold between six and eight quarts, and each family would construct great numbers of them in anticipation of harvesting sap from several hundred trees.

During the Maple Moon of early spring, entire villages emptied to set up camp in the sugar bush (akin to the old legends!) to both work and celebrate the season. Iroquois tradition included filling the mokuks with intricately designed sugar cakes and performing a maple dance when the hard work was done.

To collect as much sap as possible, the sugar gatherers would break off limbs and severely slash trunks up to four inches (10 cm) deep and nine inches (23 cm) wide in a crude V- or Y-shape, then wedge a reed or concave piece of bark in the notch to direct the flow into the mokuk. In addition to slashing sugar maple, they scored black maple, red maple, walnut, hickory, box elder, butternut, birch, sycamore, and basswood trees.

After two seasons of such treatment, however, the trees would die, and the harvesters would simply move to another portion of their inexhaustible forest. Since the forests were constantly renewing themselves, nothing was permanently lost and much valuable sugar was gained in the short run.

The earliest known container for collecting sap is the mokuk, *made of birch bark and sealed with pine resin.*

STORING THE SUGAR

These early harvesters would drink the runny sap as a sweet tonic or use it in their cooking, but had little further use for it, as it soon spoiled. They would keep some of the sap in mokuks and transfer the rest to hollowed-out logs or vats made from moose skins. If it froze, they'd simply toss off the ice and boil the remaining, now more concentrated, sweet sap.

Because the bark containers could not be placed over a fire, stones were heated in the fire and then dropped directly into the sap to boil it. A steady stream of incoming hot rocks kept the sap steaming while cooler stones were removed and cycled

Indians gathering sap

back through the fire. In later times, a soapstone bowl or a kettle of clay or iron suspended over the fire shortened both the labor and time required to thicken the sap into syrup.

The Indians would continue to boil the syrup until most of the moisture evaporated to make one of three kinds of dry sugar, which was a much more durable and portable commodity. Pouring syrup on snow made a taffylike *wax sugar*, stirring the extra-thick syrup in a mokuk crystallized it into *cake sugar*, and beating the dry remnants made a coarse and granulated *grain sugar*, similar in texture to today's brown cane sugar.

These forms of sugar allowed men to take the treat with them for use as food during long winter hunts or as valuables for bartering. Each member of the tribe could carry a personal supply in a convenient neck pouch or leather drawstring bag as a prized and vital part of his or her diet. Indeed, one anthropological study of human remains from the Woodland period estimated that an adult Lenape Indian may have eaten up to a pound of maple sugar a day!

Boiling sap in a wooden trough

> *Can it be that thou art so simple as to ask me such a question, seeing that the Master of Life has imparted to us an instinct which enables us to substitute stone hatchets and knives for those made of steel by the whites; wherefore should we not have known as well as they how to manufacture sugar? He has made us all, that we should enjoy life; he has placed before us all the requisites for the support of existence, food, water, fire, trees, etc.; wherefore then should he have withheld from us the art of excavating the trees in order to make troughs of them, of placing sap in these, of heating the stones and throwing them into the sap so as to cause it to boil, and by this means reducing it to sugar."*

KICKAPOO CHIEF JOSÉ RENARD, upon being questioned whether Indians had made maple sugar prior to contact with white men, 1824

ENJOYING THE BOUNTY

Different tribes used maple products in different ways. Both the Potawatomi and Ojibwa drank the sap straight from the tap. The Iroquois added water and black raspberries or thimbleberries to the sap to concoct a nonalcoholic drink consumed during longhouse rituals. They also fermented the sap to make alcohol and used the sugar to make beer. The sap could also be turned into vinegar, which the Potawatomi used for cooking venison (before sweetening it with maple sugar).

The Meskwaki used the syrup instead of salt to season meat and other foods. The Apache, Chiricahua, and Mescalero tribes scraped the inner bark of box elder to dry and save for winter food. Some tribes boiled the inner bark to extract its hidden sugar. Iroquois women peeled, dried, pounded, and sifted the bark of sugar maples and red maples to bake it into bread. And in a unique blending, the Cheyenne mixed box elder sap with shavings from the inner sides of animal hides for a chewy type of candy.

OTHER TREASURES OF THE TREE

Besides concocting delectable food and drink — sweet to both body and soul — the resourceful tribes devised a wealth of other uses for the versatile maple.

COMMERCE

Making sugar for domestic consumption was not the only prized use of the magnificent maple among Native Americans. Some of the more enterprising tribes manufactured cakes of maple sugar as a commercial venture — trade in the commodities market with people living outside the trees' range provided a great influx of goods to the local economy.

DYES

The Omaha and Winnebago tribe members stripped twigs and bark from the silver maple, which they roasted with iron-stained clay and tallow to make a black dye used in leather working.

WOOD

All the Woodland tribes carved the maple's hard, close-grained wood into bowls, cooking stirrers, canoe paddles, axe handles, and many other useful implements. The Micmac were known for their bows and arrows fashioned from sugar maple wood. And of course the trees contributed long-burning fuel to cooking and warming fires.

The gifts of the living trees also extended to herbal remedies for a great variety of ailments prescribed by the medicine men. A sampling:

- A poultice of outer bark for sore eyes (Micmac, Malecite)
- A compound of roots and bark for internal bleeding (Iroquois)
- A poultice of boiled root chips applied to wounds and abscesses (Algonquin)
- Pith used to remove foreign matter from eyes (Ojibwa)
- A compound of striped maple for spitting up blood (Penobscot)
- A cough suppressant made from inner bark (Mohican, Potawatomi)
- An emetic from inner bark (Meskwaki, Ojibwa)
- An expectorant (Potawatomi)
- An extract from striped maple for bronchial troubles (Abnaki); to ease shortness of breath in forest runners (Iroquois)
- A medicinal tea of steeped bark applied to swollen limbs (Penobscot)
- An infusion of red maple bark for cramps, dysentery (Cherokee); as an eyewash (Ojibwa)
- A remedy for "ballgame sickness" — back or limb pains; also sores and hemorrhoids (Seminole)

In many Native legends, each of the thirteen moons of the year offers its own benevolence. According to the Anishinaabe, the third full moon, the Maple Moon, shines during the only time of the year the sap flows from the maple trees.

HOW MAPLE SUGAR CAME TO BE
AN ANISHINAABE LEGEND

After Nanahboozhoo had given the Wild Roses their thorns, he wandered about the world playing pranks on the Little People of Darkness. They determined to have revenge on him by killing his old grandmother, Nokomis. Nanahboozhoo loved his grandmother dearly, and when he learned that the Little People wished to hurt her, he took Nokomis upon his strong back and flew away with her to a forest.

Wonderful was the forest, for it was in the autumn, and the Maple trees were all yellow, green, and crimson. From a distance it looked like a great fire and when the Little People followed after Nanahboozhoo, they thought the whole world was in flames and turned back and hid in their holes. Nanahboozhoo was so pleased with the beautiful Maples that he decided to live among them, and he made old Nokomis a wigwam of their brightest branches.

One day, some Indians came seeking Nanahboozhoo to ask for help. They found him in his grandmother's wigwam, where he received them kindly. "O Nanahbooz-hoo," said they, "the Indians of the Far South have a delicious sweet thing they call sugar, and we have nothing of the kind. We sent runners with gifts to the South to get sugar, but the people would not trade. Tell us, therefore, O Nanahboozhoo, how we may make sugar for ourselves."

At first Nanahboozhoo was puzzled, for he knew how hard it was to make sugar. But old Nokomis added her pleadings to theirs, for she too had tasted sugar and longed for more. Nanahboozhoo thought a while, and then said, "Since the beautiful Maples were so good to Nokomis, henceforth in the spring of the year they shall give the Indians sweet sap. And when the sap is boiled down thick and delicious, it will cool and harden into sugar."

Then Nanahboozhoo gave the Indians a bucket made of birch bark and a stone tapping-gouge with which to make holes in the tree trunks; and he shaped for them some cedar spouts, to put in the holes, through which the sap might run from the trees into buckets. He told them that they must build great fireplaces in the woods near the Maple groves, and when the buckets were full of sap, they must pour it into their kettles and boil it down.

And so it is that every springtime, when the frost is going out of the ground and the arbutus blossoms under the snow, the sweet sap mounts through the trunks of the Maple trees, and the Northern Indians gather the sap, and say, "This is the way Nanahboozhoo taught us to make Maple Sugar!"

— ADAPTED FROM WWW.FIRSTPEOPLE.US

YE OLDE
CONFECTIONARY
CRAFT

hen the first colonists arrived on the shores of long-established settlements of the native people, they initiated an awkward and prolonged period of getting-to-know-you. The Native Americans cautiously noted the foreigners' strange customs, odd dress, and pallid complexions. They thought it quite bewildering that these new arrivals, often insufferably dirty and with furry faces, appeared more like animals than men! The modesty-minded boat people were disturbed by the scanty garments of the New World residents and were quite put off by their liberal applications of fish oil and bear grease on their exposed flesh in wintertime to insulate themselves from the cold.

> 66 *The Sugar-Tree yields a kind of Sap or Juice which by boiling is made into Sugar. This Juice is drawn out, by wounding the Trunk of the Tree, and placing a Receiver under the Wound. It is said that the Indians make one Pound of Sugar out of eight Pounds of the Liquor. It is bright and moist with a full large Grain, the Sweetness of it being like that of good Muscovada."*

GOVERNOR BERKELEY OF VIRGINIA, 1706

LEARNING TO LIVE TOGETHER

Despite the cultural shock to both sides in those early years, each group contributed to the other's welfare. Surprisingly incompetent and ill-prepared for farming, hunting, and homesteading in the wilderness, the new arrivals nonetheless brought and made a dazzling array of valuable and beautiful goods, from copper kettles and iron axes to colorful glass — unlike anything the native people had seen before — which they gladly exchanged for seemingly cheap and mundane items, such as skinned furs.

In turn, the Native Americans taught the newcomers how to grow corn, squash, and beans together, which they planted with a small fish for fertilizer. They introduced a tea made from the fuzzy berries of the staghorn sumac, rich in vitamin C, which cured the newcomers' scurvy. And, most important for our story, they revealed the sweet treasure from the trees — unheard of in Europe — and shared the process of obtaining it.

At first, the settlers slashed the trees deeply, native-style, but they soon realized that a couple of boreholes made with an iron auger produced an acceptable flow of sap that could be more easily managed and captured. This method had the added advantage of not killing the trees after only a year or two. Instead of using pieces of bark or reeds inserted into the gash to direct the flow away from the trunk, they fashioned wooden tubes, or *spiles*, from hollow segments of elderberry, cedar, or sumac twigs.

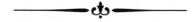

"If they are pressed by thirst, they get juice from trees and distil a sweet and very agreeable liquid, which I have tasted several times."

MARC LESCARBOT, *HISTOIRE DE LA NOUVELLE FRANCE*, 1609

STAGHORN SUMAC

The staghorn sumac is a common wayside shrub, distinctive for its thick, fuzzy twigs and upright clusters of fuzzy red berries. Not to be confused with poison sumac — which is an entirely different plant, with white berries — red staghorn sumac berries are rich in vitamin C and are relished by mice, ruffed grouse, pheasants, bobwhites, and many songbirds. The branches reminded the earliest British colonists of the antlered buck in velvet, hence the name.

Native Americans used the berries to make a tart and refreshing tea, and such a tea can still take the edge off a hot afternoon. In summer, pick a generous handful of fresh berries, drop them into a pot, and mash them slightly. Cover with boiling water and allow them to steep until the water is well colored. Strain through two thicknesses of cloth to remove the fine hairs; sweeten to taste and serve hot or cold.

Sumac spile in use

REFINING THE TECHNIQUE

In the early days, the Native Americans shared their woodland survival skills and maple sugaring know-how with the ill-prepared and naive early European pioneers. They, in turn, with their large kettles and iron tools, contributed to refining and simplifying the mutually prized product of the maple. At first, the settlers simply placed wooden buckets on the ground below the tree taps, but this still resulted in unnecessary spillage and loss, until someone figured out that the bucket could hang from a notch cut on the tightly fit spile.

Because sap will spoil if left too long in warm weather, collecting the outflow was a necessary daily chore. A strong back and a wooden neck yoke permitted transport of two bucketfuls at a time, or, if available, ox- or horse-drawn sledges with wooden

European colonists introduced the iron cauldron for boiling sap.

tanks made the daily rounds into the sugar bush. The take was then transferred to large wooden cisterns made of ash or poplar for storage until boiling.

It took a good portion of the day to visit each tap on each tree, so most of the boiling work was performed in the evenings by firelight. A large cast-iron cauldron suspended over a crackling fire, most often from a tripod lashed together from three long spars, could accommodate 20 to 30 gallons at a time. To control boiling over, the hot sap was treated with small pine boughs, bits of fat, or small quantities of heavy cream, which also introduced a subtle flavor to the finished product.

Draft horses carrying harvested sap

OF AN ATTEMPT TO MAKE
THE MAPLE SUGAR
ABOVE AN HUNDRED YEARS AGO

London, March 10, 1684

Dear Sir,

I have enclosed you some sugar of the first boiling got from the juice of the wounded maple: Mr. Ashton, Secretary to The Royal Society, presented it to me. Twas sent from Canada, where the natives prepare it from the said juice; eight pints yielding commonly a pound of sugar. The Indians have practiced it time out of mind; the French begin to refine it; and to turn it to much advantage. If you have any of these trees by you, could you not make the trial proceeding as with the sugar cane?

Dr. Robinson

Black Notley, Essex, England, April 1, 1684

Yours of the 10th instant I received, and therein an enclosed specimen of the Canada sugar, a thing to me strange and before unheard of. It were well worth the experiment you mention. I therefore engaged a friend and neighbour of mine, and ingenious apothecary, whom I employed yesterday to boil the juice of the greater maple, a tree which grows freely half a mile off from me residence. Having made an extract, we found a whitish substance, like to brown sugar, and tasting very sweet, immersed in a substance of the color and consistency of molasses. Upon curing, I have no doubt it will make perfect sugar. When it is cured, I will give you a farther account of it.

Mr. Ray

— EXCERPTED FROM *PHILOSOPHICAL MAGAZINE*, VOL. 1, ISSUE 3, 1798

"MODERN" ADVANCES

Despite its seasonality, the availability and condition of maple trees, and the intensive labor and time demanded to produce it, maple sugar was considered a necessity in the colonial diet. Imported white cane sugar was extremely expensive and hard to come by, so sugar production became a vital part of the home farm. For more than 200 years, virtually all of the sap collected in North America was processed into sugar, as no container had yet been devised to adequately store syrup over an extended period without it spoiling.

In the 1860s, an important technological advance helped push maple syrup production to its all-time peak: the nation's steel mills began to produce sheet metal, which was soon used in applications far and wide. A major development for food preservation in general was the invention of the tin can, which could store and

➤ A POLITICAL ISSUE ◄

As shown by the quotes below, maple sugar became a political issue as the abolitionist movement grew. Because the cane sugar industry relied on slave trafficking and labor, using a locally harvested resource became a way to take a stand against the exploitation of humans.

66 *Prepare for making maple sugar, which is more pleasant and patriotic than that ground by the hand of slavery, and boiled down by the heat of misery. . . . Make your own sugar and send not to the Indies for it. Feast not on the toil, pain and misery of the wretched.*

— *FARMER'S ALMANAC, 1803*

66 *Stick to the maple and so long as the maple forests stand, suffer not your cup to be sweetened by the blood of slaves!*

— *VERMONT ALMANAC, 1844*

keep food from spoiling for a long time. The new technology was a boon to sugar makers who could now preserve syrup for year-round consumption.

Sheet metal also provided the means to fashion buckets with lids to keep out rain, snow, and debris, as well as flat-bottomed shallow pans that permitted much faster sap evaporation. These wide, flat evaporating pans improved the efficiency of the "three-pot method" — still the basic process in use in today's modern evaporators. The raw sap was placed in a large pot or pan over heat. As the sap darkened in color and began to sweeten, it was ladled into another pan. As the sap continued to evaporate, it was ladled once again into a third pot for finishing into syrup.

Such an operation deserved its own dedicated shelter constructed in the wooded valley (all the better for carrying the heavy sap from the trees); hence, the sugar shack, another innovation whose use continues today.

The invention of sheet metal introduced the now iconic sap bucket made from tin.

Perhaps part of the enduring appeal of maple sugaring, in addition to the delicious end product, is the contrast between the still-frozen winter landscape and the steamy, sweet-smelling sugarhouse.

PREPARING FOR THE SEASON

The colonial family began preparing for the annual sugaring season weeks before the actual rising of the sap. Children would harvest sumac or elderberry twigs to make the spiles. After cutting them into lengths of about eight inches (20 cm), they would burn out the soft center pith with a hot iron poker and taper one end to fit into the borehole. Buckets were assembled and cleaned.

When the days warmed the landscape and snow began to melt, yet nights still remained frigid, it was time to take all the spiles and buckets the family owned out to the sugar stand. After placing a spile and bucket at the base of each maple, the men or boys would follow with the auger, drill a hole, tap in the spile, and place the bucket.

But for this procedure to work, everyone had to be able to correctly identify the maple trees in their winter appearances. It does no good to waste time and effort tapping an oak tree! In the next chapter, we'll look at the maple's family tree.

FAMILY TREE

GALLERY

If not for its distinctive characteristics, the sugar-producing maple would be just an ordinary tree of the mountains, hills, and valleys. And so it is for folks who never notice the trees for the woods.

The maple genus (*Acer*) encompasses 124 species, 78 subspecies, and 8 varieties of trees and shrubs at home throughout the northern temperate world. The maple epitomizes tree perfection — it is well-proportioned, symmetrical, strong, handsome, and elegant. Most members share the family characteristics of deciduous, palmate (hand-shaped, in nontechnical terms) leaves; balanced, opposite branches; minute, intricate flowers; and wind-borne, two-winged seeds; but only a few produce sweet sap. Of those, all but one (the Norway, which commercial sugarmakers don't use) are native to North America.

The sugar maple, *Acer saccharum*, is perhaps the most beautiful and functional of all. Standing alone, the silhouette of the tree forms a nearly perfect oval; its sleek

and graceful seeds are engineered to aerodynamic precision. Its bright, fine-grained, hardwood polishes to a peerless luster in many fine applications; as firewood, it burns evenly without sparks and fits, presents pleasant colors and fragrance, and releases great stores of energy. And the leaves are geometrical masterpieces that, in autumn, rival the sunset itself for color ablaze.

The maple's distinctive winged seeds whirling through the air in the fall are a familiar sight in many parts of North America.

HOW TO IDENTIFY A MAPLE

Most maple groves consist of just one variety of maple. The sugar maple, with its highest content of sugar, is the first preference for the sugar farmer or backyard do-it-yourselfer when it comes to making maple syrup. The black, red, and silver maples, however, can also be used, as can the box elder. (Box elder is the odd-looking member — there's one in every family!)

The easiest way to identify a maple is with a casual glance at its familiar hand-shaped leaves; however, their complete absence in late winter/early spring forces us to look more closely for other reliable identifying characteristics.

Looking at the bark (generally a smooth gray-brown color that fissures and cracks vertically as the tree grows in girth), we must really know our stuff, for other trees have similar skins. We may also examine the buds, for although a tree may be dormant in winter, it issues its buds the previous fall in preparation for another growing season. Each species boasts its own variation; see tree descriptions on pages 44 to 57 for details.

BY ITS BRANCHES YE SHALL KNOW IT

We can also look to its pattern of branching, which is perhaps the best method for narrowing our winter identification. Maples grow their branches in an arrangement slightly different from most other trees of the forest: Wherever there's a branch, or twig, or bud, you'll find it matched with a twin on its opposite side. This is called, appropriately enough, *opposite branching*. (Most trees have *alternate branching* in which limbs sprout at intervals apart; some trees' branches whorl in all directions as they issue outward.)

In the Northeast, just three other common trees have opposite branching, but they are unmistakably different from the maple in such other traits as size, overall shape, bark, twigs, buds, and leaves. The way to remember these four is to think of the acronym MAD HORSE: Maple, Ash, Dogwood, Horse Chestnut.

The maple tree's opposite branching is a helpful way to identify one in the winter.

If you don't want to be skulking around in the dead of winter squinting at twig ends in dim afternoon light, think ahead and be observant. While the weather remains favorable and the trees are still wearing their leaves like so many "Hello, My Name Is . . ." badges, simply tie a string of remembrance around the trunk for when you later return.

AN ILLUSTRATED FAMILY TREE

There are thirteen maple species native to North America that can be tapped by the hobbyist, as can the Norway maple, an introduced species. Maple trees can be found throughout the land, not just in the Northeast and Canada. The members of the Maple family Aceraceae are more widespread than many folks realize. Get to know them well if you can.

The illustrated portraits in the following pages feature the seven most common syrup-producing members of the maple family, in order of sugar production: Sugar Maple, Black Maple, Red Maple, Silver Maple, Box Elder, Norway Maple, and Bigleaf Maple.

The sugar and black maples produce the most sap with the highest concentration of sugar. The sap from other trees needs to be boiled longer to produce syrup.

A MERCIFULLY BRIEF GLOSSARY

Lenticels SMALL PORES ON WOODY PLANTS THAT ALLOW GASES TO PASS TO AND FROM THE INTERIOR TISSUES; APPEAR LIKE LITTLE SPOTS ON TWIGS

Margin THE BORDER OF A LEAF

Palmate HAVING LOBES OR LEAFLETS RADIATING FROM ONE POINT; RESEMBLING AN OPEN HAND

Samara WINGED, ONE-SEEDED FRUIT; MAPLES HAVE PAIRED SAMARAS

THIRTEEN NATIVE MAPLES

Species	Native Habitat
Bigleaf Maple* (*ACER MACROPHYLLUM*)	PACIFIC COAST OF THE UNITED STATES AND CANADA
Black Maple* (*A. SACCHARUM SSP. NIGRUM*)	NORTHEASTERN UNITED STATES AND SOUTHEASTERN CANADA
Box Elder* (*A. NEGUNDO*)	EASTERN AND CENTRAL UNITED STATES AND CANADA
Canyon Maple (*A. SACCHARUM SSP. GRANDIDENTATUM*)	U.S. ROCKY MOUNTAINS
Chalk Maple (*A. SACCHARUM VAR. LEUCODERME*)	SOUTHEASTERN UNITED STATES
Florida Maple (*A. × ROTUNDILOBUM*)	SOUTHEASTERN U.S. COASTAL PLAIN AND PIEDMONT
Mountain Maple (*A. SPICATUM*)	NORTHEASTERN UNITED STATES AND SOUTHEASTERN CANADA
Red Maple* (*A. RUBRUM*)	EASTERN UNITED STATES AND SOUTHEASTERN CANADA
Rocky Mountain Maple (*A. GLABRUM*)	WESTERN UNITED STATES
Silver Maple* (*A. SACCHARINUM*)	EASTERN UNITED STATES AND SOUTHEASTERN CANADA
Striped Maple (*A. PENSYLVANICUM*)	NORTHEASTERN UNITED STATES AND SOUTHEASTERN CANADA
Sugar Maple* (*A. SACCHARUM*)	NORTHEASTERN UNITED STATES AND SOUTHEASTERM CANADA
Vine Maple (*A. CIRCINATUM*)	PACIFIC COAST OF UNITED STATES AND CANADA

*These six are profiled in following illustrations, as is the Norway maple, an introduced species.
They are the most commonly tapped by hobbyists.

Sugar Maple

A.K.A. ROCK MAPLE, HARD MAPLE

Acer saccharum

Sugar content   3–5%

Mature height   60–100 feet (18–30 m)

The spectacular sugar maple is a sturdy and long-lived specimen (more than 200 years) that grows best in deep, moist, well-drained soils. Its blazing autumn foliage and high-sugar-content sap make it one of the most well-known and respected trees in the world.

LEAVES

* 5 lobes (rarely 3), U-shaped between lobes
* 3–6 inches (7.5–15 cm)
* Bright green above, paler below
* Smooth margin
* Fall: yellow, bright red-orange

BARK

* Young: smooth, grayish brown
* Older: darker, ridged with thick, irregularly curled plates that appear to peel from the trunk in a vertical direction

TWIGS
* Reddish brown to light brown
* Slender and shiny with lighter lenticels

BUDS
* ¼–3/8-inch (0.6–0.9 cm)
* Brown, narrow, sharply pointed, with tight scales

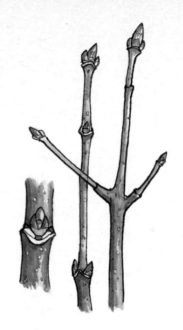

FLOWERS
* Small
* Hang from 1–3 inch (2.5–7.5 cm) stem in clusters
* Light yellowish green
* Appear with/before leaves in spring

FRUIT
* Clusters of green horseshoe-shaped paired samaras on a stalk
* Wings ½–1 inch (1.25–2.5 cm)
* Matures brown in fall

Black Maple

Acer saccharum ssp. *nigrum*
Sugar content   3–5%
Mature height   50–100 feet (15–30 m)

The black maple is very similar to the sugar maple and was for a time considered its subspecies. Although it occupies a smaller range than the sugar, distinguishing between the two types is not crucial because they are essentially identical in quality as sugar trees.

LEAVES

* Usually 3, occasionally 5 lobes, smooth margin
* 3–6 inches (7.5–15 cm); thicker than sugar maple leaves
* Downy below
* Tend to droop and curl
* Fall: bright yellow

BARK

* Young: smooth, dark gray to black
* Older: scaly or with long, thick, irregular ridges

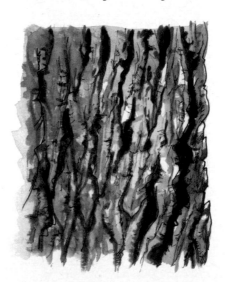

TWIGS

* Slender brown to orange with
  light lenticels

BUDS

* Brown, plump
* Sharply pointed

FLOWERS

* Small
* Hang from 1–3 inch (2.5–
  7.5 cm) stem in clusters
* Light yellowish green
* Appear with leaves in spring

FRUIT

* Clusters of green horseshoe-
  shaped paired samaras on a
  stalk
* Wings ½–1 inch (1.25–2.5 cm)
* Matures brown in fall

Red Maple

A.K.A. SWAMP MAPLE, SCARLET MAPLE

Acer rubrum

Sugar content   2–3.5%

Mature height   40–90 feet (12–27 m)

Red maple is one of the most abundant and widespread hardwood trees in North America, thriving on a wide variety of soils, from swamps to dry ridges. Some part of the tree displays its signature color during each season: spring, flowers; summer, leaf stems; fall, leaves; winter, buds and twig ends.

LEAVES

* 3–5 lobes, V-shaped between lobes
* 2–4 inches (5–10 cm)
* Serrated margin
* Green above, sometimes pale or hairy below
* Fall: crimson to yellow

BARK

* Young: smooth, light gray
* Older: darker gray with long scaly ridges

TWIGS
* Shiny red with numerous light lenticels
* V-shaped leaf scars

BUDS
* Green or reddish
* Blunt

FLOWERS
* Round, bright red clusters
* Appear early spring before leaves

FRUIT
* Slightly divergent paired samaras on slim stems
* Reddish brown
* Wings ½–¾ inch (1.25–1.9 cm)
* Matures late spring/summer

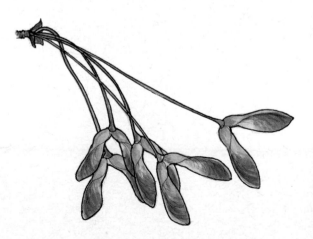

Silver Maple

A.K.A. SOFT MAPLE

Acer saccharinum

Sugar content   2–2.5%

Mature height   50–100+ feet (15–30 m)

The silver maple, often planted as an ornamental, is a fast-growing tree with a fondness for floodplains and other moist soils. Its short trunk typically splits into several subtrunks whose mature diameter can exceed 3 feet (1 m). Long slender branches arch downward then curve gracefully upward.

LEAVES
* 5 deeply cut lobes
* Coarsely serrated margin
* 5–7 inches (13–18 cm)
* Light green above, silvery-white below
* Fall: yellow to brown

BARK
* Young: smooth, silvery gray
* Older: broken into long, loose, narrow strips

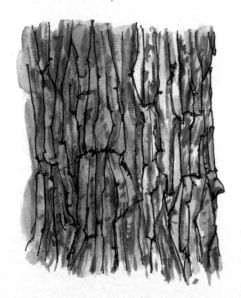

TWIGS
* Green in early spring, turning orangish brown, with many light-colored lenticels

BUDS
* Small, reddish brown with large scales
* Pointed
* Near twig ends

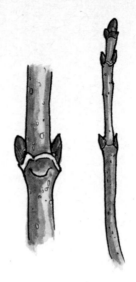

FLOWERS
* Separate male and female flowers on the same tree
* Greenish to reddish dense clusters below leaf buds
* Appear early spring long before leaves

FRUIT
* Large green paired samaras
* Wings 1½–2½ inches (3.8–6 cm) curving inward
* Matures brown late spring, and germinates upon release

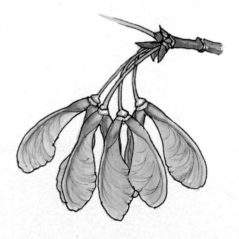

Box Elder

A.K.A. ASHLEAF MAPLE, MANITOBA MAPLE, CALIFORNIA BOX ELDER

Acer negundo

Sugar content   1.5–2%

Mature height   40–60 feet (12–18 m)

The only species of maple with a compound leaf, the box elder is the most wide-spread and tolerant of environmental conditions. It also has the softest wood and, with weedy-looking shoots sprouting from multiple trunks, has the least aesthetic appearance in the family. Of little, if any, commercial use, its sap is nonetheless sweet enough for processing by the backyard syrup maker.

LEAVES

* 3–5 leaflets, coarsely serrated margin
* 2–4 inches (5–10 cm)
* Light green above, paler below
* Similar to poison ivy
* Fall: pale yellow

BARK

* Young: light brown to gray, warty
* Older: shallow interconnected ridges

TWIGS

* Pastel red, green to purplish green
* Often coated with soft white powder that rubs off, glossy underneath

BUDS

* White, hairy
* Large-scaled, blunt

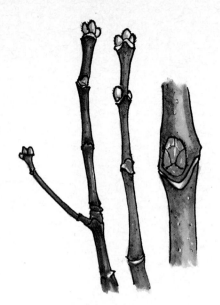

FLOWERS

* Yellowish green in hanging clusters along a single axis
* Male and female flowers on separate trees
* Appear in spring

FRUIT

* V-shaped, green, paired samaras in drooping clusters
* Wings 1–1½ inch (2.5–3.8 cm)
* Matures light tan in fall

Norway Maple

Acer platanoides
Sugar content   1.5–2%
Mature height   50–80 feet (15–24 m)

The Norway maple is a nonnative species from Europe that has been planted extensively as an ornamental street and shade tree for its very dense canopy. While commercial syrup producers do not generally tap the Norway because of the availability and number of other more productive trees, its stature in the backyard makes it worthwhile for the hobbyist.

LEAVES
* 5–7 lobes, U-shaped between lobes
* 4½–8 inches (11–20 cm)
* Milky sap exudes from broken leaf stem
* Dark green above, paler below; or purple-black (Crimson King variety)
* Fall: red, maroon

BARK
* Young: smooth, light brown
* Older: dark brown, long narrow, interconnected ridges

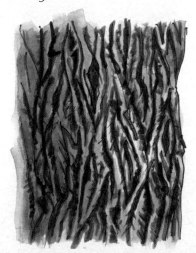

TWIGS
* Stout, reddish brown

BUDS
* Blunt
* Green to purple
* Turban-shaped end bud much larger than side ones
* Large scales have keel-like ridges

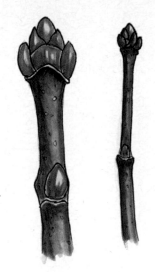

FLOWERS
* Separate male and female flowers on same tree
* Bright yellowish green
* Appear early spring before leaves

FRUIT
* Green
* Widely spread, paired samaras
* Wings 1½–3 inches (3.8–7.5 cm)
* Relatively flat seed cavity
* Matures late summer/fall

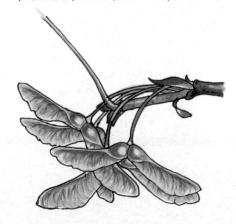

Bigleaf Maple

A.K.A. BROADLEAF MAPLE, OREGON MAPLE

Acer macrophyllum

Sugar content   1.5–2%

Mature height   40–100+ feet (12–30 m)

Of the native maples that produce sap sweet enough to tap, the bigleaf maple is the largest of the entire family. It is a vigorous stump-sprouter and one of the few commercial hardwoods native to the Pacific coast; its large burls are highly desirable for furniture veneers. In the open, it branches low to the ground and forms a rounded crown.

LEAVES

* 5 deep lobes
* Terminal lobe has distinct "waist"
* 6–12 inches (15–30 cm)
* Dark green above, light green below
* Leaf stem exudes milky sap
* Fall: yellow, orangish brown

BARK

* Young: smooth, grayish brown
* Older: darker brown with interconnecting ridges

TWIGS
* Smooth, stout
* Pale to bright green or red

BUDS
* Stout, larger terminal bud
* 3–4 reddish green scales

FLOWERS
* Small, yellow, in hanging clusters along a single axis
* Separate male and female flowers on same or different trees
* Appear early spring

FRUIT
* V-shaped, pale green, paired samaras in clusters
* Wings 1½–2 inches (4–5 cm) with hairy seed heads
* Matures tan in fall

SEASONS OF THE SUGAR BUSH

"Each phase of nature, while not invisible, is not yet too distinct and obtrusive. It is there to be found when we look for it, but not demanding our attention."

These words, written by Henry David Thoreau in 1858, aptly describe the seasons of the sugar bush. Although spring is the busiest time, it can be said that the maple season officially begins on January first and ends on December thirty-first. Between those days lie all of the sugarer's passions, pursuits, and pleasures.

SPRING

The crows' lusty cries herald the coming of spring — though the calendar may yet deny it — as frosty nights and mild days signal the start of the sugaring season. Rising external temperatures draw the sap upward to jump-start new growth at the twigs' ends until the new leaves begin food production. Riding that flow is a reserve of last year's leftover — yet still potent — sugar food. Although comprising less than five percent of the sap, that sugar is the trees' internal link to a sustainable future, as it feeds the growth of new leaves until they are large enough to take over the production of fuel.

The sugar farmer and helpers of all ages turn out to tap the trees, gather the clear sap, and assist with the harvest. Although the sap flow varies with the weather, and taps may produce for 6 to 8 weeks, the majority of the sap is collected in a 10- to 14-day "sap run." Collecting continues until the weather warms up and the sap stops running, but an entire season may last only two weeks if there's a fast transition from winter to spring!

As the interior temperature of the tree reaches about 45°F (7°C), buds open, leaves begin to develop and spread, the sap loses its sweetness, becomes slightly milky, and stops running, signaling the end of the brief but glorious sugar season. The last of the collected sap is boiled down for a darker grade of syrup and packaged for sale and shipping — along with all the other syrups, creams, sugars, candies, and maple products. The sweet satisfaction of a job well done comes only after all the equipment is thoroughly cleaned and stored for next year.

Maple is the wood of choice for bowling alleys and dance floors.

SUMMER

Minuscule food factories filled with quadrillions of chlorophyll molecules manufacture sugar in shifts that last as long as the daylight. The production of sugar, which fuels the growth of leaves, fruits, seeds, bark, and wood, outpaces the trees' ability to use it. What isn't immediately consumed is converted to starch and stashed in the trunk and roots for later use, some of which will be tapped for harvest nine to ten months later.

In the canopies, birds, insects, and mammals find food, water, and cover. The living sugar bush habitat supports wildlife populations, cleanses polluted air, filters and stores rainwater and runoff, prevents soil erosion, protects the watershed, and maintains crucial biodiversity of native species.

Syrup producers sell their maple products, plan new marketing strategies and production improvements, dream of new equipment, and hope for a best-ever season next spring.

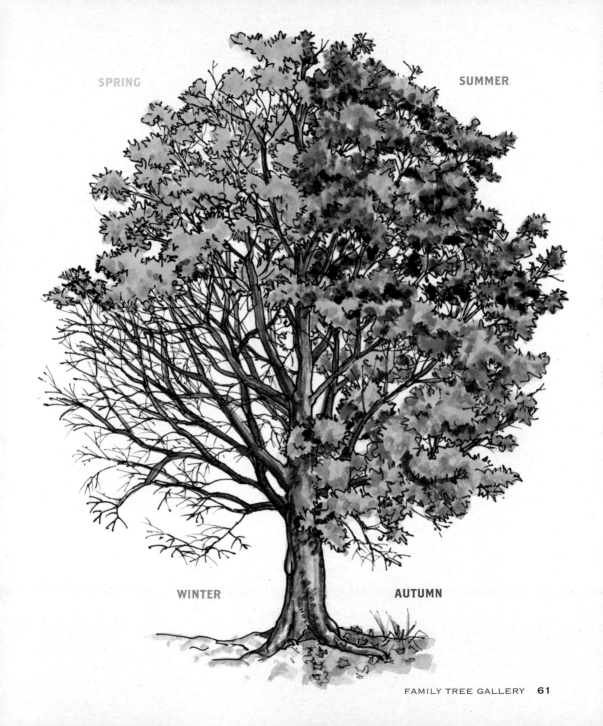

SPRING

SUMMER

WINTER

AUTUMN

AUTUMN

With the decrease of sunlight during autumn, cork cells invade the stems of the leaves and shut off the water supply to the food factories. As the chlorophyll desiccates, photosynthesis ceases and the tree enters dormancy for the winter to conserve water and energy. New buds form and await their unveiling with the advent of longer days. As the green of the chlorophyll vanishes, the remaining pigments in the leaves show their true colors.

In a remarkable season finale, these formerly hidden hues become the dominant eye-catchers. The yellow pigment, one of the xanthophylls; orange carotene pigments; and the deep reds and purples of anthocyanins combine in billions of one-of-a-kind leaf-sized masterpieces.

Each tree displays its own cloak of color: the flaming reddish orange and yellow of the sugar maples; the scarlet of the red maples; the burnished gold of the black maples; the paler yellows of the silver maples and box elders; and the deep maroons of the Norway maples.

The leaves succumb to wind and gravity, adding their spent bodies to the fertile humus of the forest floor. In time, their nutrients reduce to basic elements and are recaptured by new growth in the eternal life cycle.

In the sugar bush, the maple farmer tends to fallen or dead trees, removes non-maple species, and restocks the supply of firewood for the evaporator.

And you, how old are you?
I asked the maple tree:
While opening one hand,
— he started blushing.

GEORGES BONNEAU, *LE
SENSIBILITÉ JAPONAISE*, 1935

WINTER

The sugar bush rests. Though the trees are dormant on the outside and cold on the inside, enzymes in the wood are actively converting stored starch into sugar as the tree awaits the trigger of longer daylight and warmer temperatures to begin again the cycle of growth and reproduction.

In years gone by, winter was a time to make the spiles for the upcoming harvest season: cutting twigs of staghorn sumac, elderberry, and cedar into short segments and burning out their innards with a hot iron poker. Modern sugar farmers use this time perform maintenance on their drills, tubing, evaporators, fireboxes, and other vital equipment. They order necessary supplies, ready advertising materials, and complete preparations for open houses, sugar bush tours, maple festivals, and other events.

———————— ♣ ————————

"A sap-run is the sweet good-by of winter.
It is the fruit of the equal marriage of the sun and frost."

JOHN BURROUGHS, *SIGNS AND SEASONS*, 1886

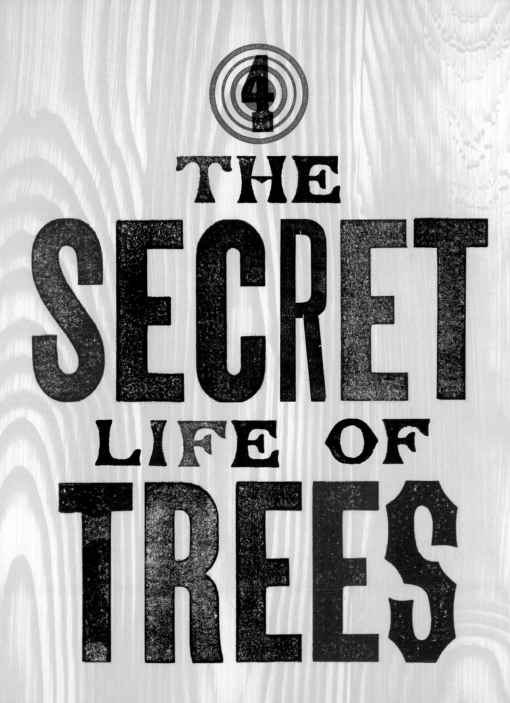

4

THE
SECRET
LIFE OF
TREES

uietly hidden inside a maple tree is an incredibly complex biochemical system of growth and development. Let's imagine we can shrink to subatomic size for a surreal voyage to the microscopic chemical laboratories inside the tree, as well as to its food production, transport, and warehousing facilities, to gain access to the thriving internal operations of a live tree without harming it in any way.

STARTING WITH SUNLIGHT

We begin our journey on a beam of sunlight, traveling at the speed of light, escorted by visible light in all its spectral glory. As we strike the leaf, we enter the receiving area of the plant, known as the *chloroplast*, where the raw materials of water, minerals, gases, and light energy are combined to manufacture carbohydrates.

We are immediately processed by special energy-absorbing molecules called *chlorophyll*. The varying wavelengths of red, orange, yellow, blue, and violet energy are all efficiently absorbed, but green is reflected, giving the molecules (and hence the leaves) their characteristic hue.

In a mature tree, all the chloroplasts combined may provide a surface area for light absorption totaling some 150 square miles.

THAT FAMOUS FLAG

Indigenous Canadian tribes were as well aware of the glories of the maple as their neighbors to the south, and they also shared their knowledge with the European settlers as they arrived. According to many historians, the maple leaf was used as a Canadian symbol as early as 1700. By 1860, the maple leaf was part of the badge of the 100th Regiment (Royal Canadians) and the maple leaf theme was used extensively in decorations for the visit of the Prince of Wales that year.

It wasn't until February 15, 1965, that it made its official appearance on the country's flag, a date celebrated annually as National Flag of Canada Day. The number and arrangement of the points of the maple leaf were chosen after wind tunnel tests showed the current design to be the least blurry of the various choices when tested under high wind conditions.

CONTINUING WITH CHLOROPHYLL

Illuminated and energized, still inside the leaf, the chlorophyll releases its energy into the water around us, splitting it into its component atoms of hydrogen and oxygen. The liberated oxygen promptly pairs up and escapes out of the leaf into the atmosphere, while the hydrogen is snapped up by carbon dioxide in a series of ongoing reactions that produce a carbohydrate and some water, in a process known as *photosynthesis*.

As food for the tree, this carbohydrate (phosphoglyceraldehyde, in case you're interested) is employed in one of several ways: 1) as a respiratory fuel to be used immediately, 2) modified for transport as a building material for construction or repair of any of the innumerable cells throughout the tree, or 3) stored for later use.

We can track these modified meals as they are sent packing. Because the original fuel is quite volatile, it would become permanently entangled with other substances long before reaching its intended destination. Therefore, it must first be neutralized into a less industrious form for transport: glucose.

GOING ON WITH GLUCOSE

Glucose is whisked away from the leaves back through the branches, trunk, and roots with the sap. Enzymes in other cells break down the sugar food and recombine it with nitrogen and other minerals to make fats, oils, and proteins, which contribute to the formation of leaves, fruits, and seeds. Some is converted into cellulose for new wood and bark construction.

As long as the sun shines on the leaf, production of glucose outpaces immediate consumption, so the bulk of glucose is further converted to starch (a quite compact and inert package) for storage in the trunk and roots. As this is our destination as well, we patiently wait there for the next growing season.

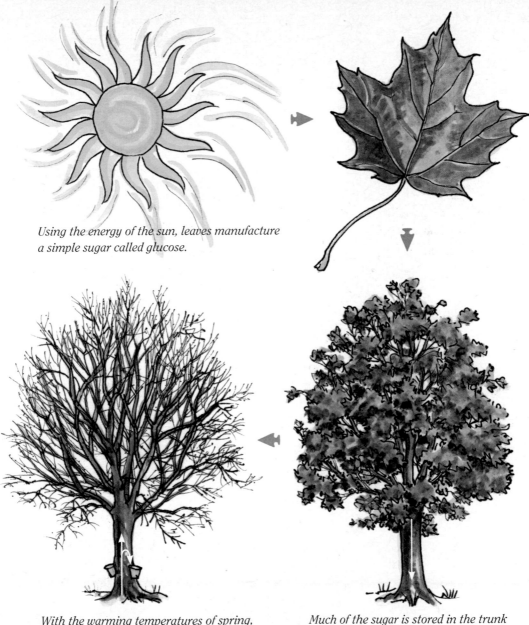

Using the energy of the sun, leaves manufacture a simple sugar called glucose.

Much of the sugar is stored in the trunk and roots during the winter.

With the warming temperatures of spring, the sugar is drawn upward to fuel the tree's growth and can be collected.

ENDING WITH ENZYMES

During fall and winter, when the temperature of the wood drops below about 40°F (4°C), enzymes reconvert the stored starches back into sugars of glucose, fructose, and sucrose, which then pass into the sap for ready use. In early spring, rising outside temperatures affect the pressure on the fluids inside the tree, which draws the sap upward to fuel new growth until this season's leaf laboratories become operational and food production is once again online.

As our virtual vessel rises with the flow in the sapwood, we suddenly find ourselves exiting the tree via a portal directly to the outside world. We splash down in a bucketful of sap and bob in a solution of one to four percent sugar, before we transform back to our original size.

As the interior temperature of the wood reaches about 45°F (7°C), the enzymes cease functioning and sugar is no longer produced in the clear, watery sap. The buds on the twigs burst open, leaves begin to unfurl, the existing sugar changes back into starch, and the sap stops flowing. The comprehensive food production, transport, and storage operation has come full cycle.

BARKING UP THE RIGHT TREE

Now that we have plumbed the depths of the intricate biochemistry of the tree, have seen some of its complex inner workings, and have obtained a prized sample of maple sap for processing, what's next? Let's take a closer look at a cross-section of the trunk, with its many layers.

A woody tissue that protects the tree from disease and injury, temperature extremes, and insects.

Transports sap laden with sugar food from the leaves downward to the branches, trunk, and roots. In late winter/early spring, this flow reverses to help nourish swelling buds and leaves.

A microscopic layer of cells specializing in division, producing new phloem to the outside and new xylem to the inside. Such growth increases the tree's girth each year and configures the annual growth rings.

Transports water, minerals, sugar food, and other nutrients upward in the tree from the roots to the twigs. The internal pressure in late winter/early spring induces a strong flow of sucrose-laden sap to fuel new growth everywhere.

Inactive xylem that has become clogged with particles and has formed dense, hard wood that gives strength to the tree. It is usually darker colored than active xylem.

Specialized cells that conduct food and water radially and that serve in food storage.

Comprised of two types of wood. The wider band of lighter-colored wood is *springwood*, formed during the moist springtime when growth is faster. The narrower, darker band is *summerwood*, grown at a slower rate during the drier summer. Count either the light or the dark rings when aging the tree: one light ring and one dark ring together account for one year's growth.

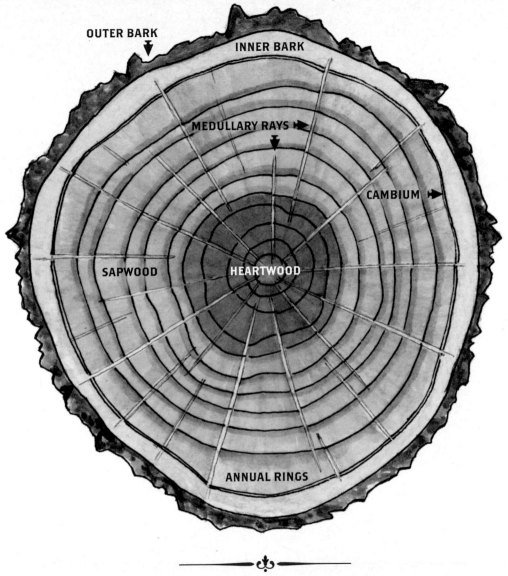

OUTER BARK

INNER BARK

MEDULLARY RAYS ▸

CAMBIUM ▸

SAPWOOD

HEARTWOOD

ANNUAL RINGS

Sugar maples can live for centuries and achieve
as much as 23 feet in girth.

5

FOR FUN, PROFIT & HARD WORK

Commercial production of maple syrup has always been an intensive labor-of-love business. It offers such perks as working outdoors (in the cold and damp); self-determining one's business potential (subject to Nature's whims) and work schedule (morning to afternoon to evening to night to morning); and offering a popular product (according to the latest research, techniques, and laws for quality and compliance).

Nonetheless, professional syrup producers are in business to make money and must look after the health and well-being of their cash crop year-round, not just at harvest time. They must invest in, maintain, and store their tools, equipment, and supplies in good and clean working order; arrange for extra workers during the busy periods; and wear all the hats of ownership, management, planning, purchasing, marketing, sales, maintenance, labor, and all-around helper.

Finally, despite all their efforts, the quantity and quality of the finished products are largely out of their control, subject to the health of the trees, the conditions and variability of the weather, and nature's transition from winter to spring (which doesn't necessarily match the calendar's!). And then there's always that nagging principle of supply and demand to mess with their bottom lines.

And yet, it's a great business — unique in history, romance, lore, purpose, technique, and location. Where else could one work so hard to refine such a tiny percentage of raw material into such a cherished delicacy? (There's always scraping the bark of *Boswellia* trees for the frankincense trade, but that's a whole different industry!)

———⚜———

But I've got to say that there is something magical
about sugarin', and if you talk with people who make maple syrup,
either in a big commercial evaporator or out in the
backyard, you'll find out there's a lot of agreement on that fact.

RINK MANN, *BACKYARD SUGARING*, 1976

A NORTH AMERICAN MAPLE TIMELINE

1540
First written observation of North American maple trees, by Jacques Cartier, a French explorer traveling up St. Lawrence River.

1606
Marc Lescarbot describes collection and "distillation" of maple sap by Micmac Indians of eastern Canada (*Histoire de la Nouvelle France*).

1788
Quakers promote the manufacture and use of maple sugar as an alternative to West Indian cane sugar produced with slave labor.

1791
A Dutch company buys 23,000 acres of Vermont land to compete with cane from West Indies. Project fails; Vermonters prefer to work their own land.

1791
Thomas Jefferson and George Washington try to start "maple orchards" on their Virginia plantations. Most trees die. Jefferson remains a maple booster.

1810
As augers come into popular use to drill holes for spiles, crude gashings or "boxing" techniques become obsolete.

1818
Maple sugar sells for half the price of imported cane sugar.

1858
Early patent for evaporating pan awarded to D. M. Cook of Ohio.

1859
Eli Mosher patents first metal sap spouts.

1860
Peak maple production year for United States: 40 million pounds of sugar and 1.6 million gallons of syrup, from 23 states reporting to USDA.

1875
Introduction of metal sap buckets.

1880
Cane sugar and maple sugar approximately equal in price.

1884
Early patent for sugar evaporator awarded to G. H. Grimm of Hudson, Ohio.

1891
McKinley Bill attempts to promote maple sugar manufacture with two-cent-per-pound bounty to producers. Wrangling ensues; effort fails.

1893
Vermont Maple Sugar Makers Association forms; is instrumental in setting industry-wide standards.

1905
U.S. Pure Food and Drug Act makes adulteration of maple syrup with glucose illegal.

1935
Vermont institutes spring Maple Festivals; 134 towns stage events; 1,200 maple-frosted cakes are submitted for judging.

1940–1945
Maple prices frozen at $3.39 per gallon during World War II. Production suffers.

1946
First commercial power-tapping machine is marketed.

1959
Plastic sap-gathering pipeline system patented by Nelson Griggs, Montpelier, Vermont.

1982
Severe local dieback or decline of sugar maples noted in Quebec. Provincial scientists begin searching for causes.

1988
North American Maple Project begins studying health of maple trees to determine progression, if any, of maple decline.

1997
Changes in sap-tubing technology offer "permanent" tubing, which can be left in the woods year-round without stretching.

1999
Introduction of the "health spout," using a smaller hole in the tree, which can be drilled by cordless drills. A smaller hole heals faster.

MODERN MAPLE SUGARING

Today's successful sugar farmer benefits from a number of laborsaving and efficiency-enhancing technologies that have elevated the commercial production of maple syrup and related products beyond the scope of most backyard hobbyists — although there's still much joy and purpose in that endeavor as well!

The roots of modern maple sugar farming operations began with the availability of sheet metal in the 1860s, which allowed for such production-increasing implements as metal-lidded sap cans, flat-bottomed evaporator pans, storage tanks, and metal spiles, as well as cans for preserving finished syrup. Later, rolled galvanized steel cans replaced tin buckets, and the brace-and-bit replaced the auger, which in turn was outmuscled by gas- and battery-operated power tappers for a much faster and easier chore.

In spite of advances such as the metal sap bucket and power drills, the basic process of gathering sap and boiling it down to make syrup remains unchanged.

The metal sap-gathering tubing invented in 1916 by W. C. Brower of Mayfield, New York, proved impractical: it was prone to freezing at night, leakage, and was vulnerable to damage by deer.

YOU STILL HAVE TO COLLECT A WHOLE LOT OF SAP

For all the improvements, the basic job remained the labor-intensive project it had always been: individually tapping hundreds of trees, hanging the buckets, and visiting each one daily to collect the sap before boiling it down. Horses and mules were often enlisted to haul sledges or wagons carrying large tanks, whose job was later mechanized by farm tractors and heavy all-terrain vehicles.

But starting in the late 1950s, advances in the plastics industry introduced a revolutionary new collection technique that enabled hundreds of trees to be interconnected with vinyl tubing. Using gravity to drain the sap downhill through a network of tubing saved the countless hours and muscle aches of daily trudging and lugging chores. Most commercial operators now use miles of tubing to harvest the sugar bush directly to a large centralized storage tank, which in turn feeds directly to the sugarhouse.

The professional sugar maker is always conscientious to minimize any potential contamination of the sap by bacteria. Drill bits, spiles, buckets, tubing, and other equipment are all kept scrupulously clean, and collected sap is prevented from warming or staying too long in the sun. When transferring sap to the storage tank, some producers use an in-line ultraviolet light to reduce the amount of living microorganisms.

→ WORKING IN A VACUUM ←

Of the farmers who use the tubing system, many also increase their yields with the use of a vacuum pump. This may sound misleading at first, because sap cannot be pulled or sucked from a tree. Nonetheless, the flow of sap in the trees is a result of higher pressure in the trees than in the atmosphere, so a vacuum pump connected to the tubing system in effect lowers the outside pressure, inducing the sap to flow more freely from the tapholes.

Sugar farmers used to collect sap in buckets that were emptied daily by hand.

Commercial farmers now use miles of tubing to drain the sap into a tank that feeds directly to the sugarhouse.

TURNING SAP INTO SYRUP

On average, it takes about 40 gallons (150 liters) of sugar maple sap to make just one gallon (3.8 liters) of syrup (and 50–70 gallons [189–265 liters] or more from other species), which means an immense amount of water must be boiled away. The backyard hobbyist can contend with a shallow pan over an open fire; those with a slightly larger operation may prefer an outdoor gas furnace that gives a more even and dependable heat to the evaporating pan. But the commercial sugar farmer, with perhaps 10,000 or more gallons of harvested sap, invests in a large evaporating machine housed in a dedicated building.

The sugar shack or sugarhouse, introduced during the late 1700s and usually slapped together in the middle of the sugar bush, has evolved into a modern production and processing facility with concrete floors, electricity, plumbing, and ventilation systems. It may have dedicated spaces for a finishing kitchen, public salesroom, and fuel storage, and is usually located for convenience and public access near the farm's other buildings.

A facility for processing maple syrup is known as a sugar shack.

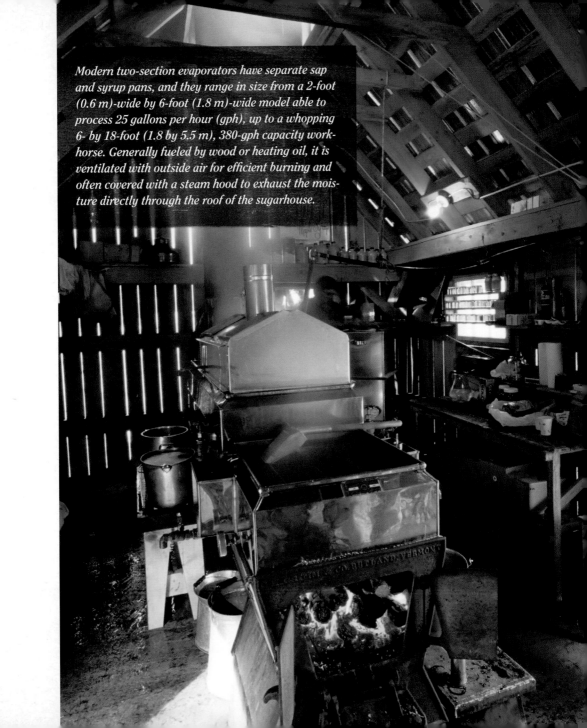

Modern two-section evaporators have separate sap and syrup pans, and they range in size from a 2-foot (0.6 m)-wide by 6-foot (1.8 m)-wide model able to process 25 gallons per hour (gph), up to a whopping 6- by 18-foot (1.8 by 5.5 m), 380-gph capacity work-horse. Generally fueled by wood or heating oil, it is ventilated with outside air for efficient burning and often covered with a steam hood to exhaust the moisture directly through the roof of the sugarhouse.

Commercial sugar farmers have large evaporating machines that produce intense heat and an immense amount of steam.

TAKING THE TEMPERATURE OF THE SAP

From a large outdoor storage tank, raw sap is admitted to the sap pan through a float valve that controls a certain depth. As the sap cooks down and the sugar concentration increases, it progresses through multiple sections of the pan before being transferred to the syrup pan through a pipe. There it proceeds through more channeled partitions as it continues to evaporate in shallow layers without the danger of burning, before reaching the last, finishing section.

Sap becomes syrup at a specific temperature, which is 7.25°F (4.2°C) above the boiling temperature of water. This is not as easy to check as you might think. Remember that water boils at less than 212°F (100°C) at higher elevations — one degree Fahrenheit less for each 550 feet (168 m) above sea level — and fluctuates according to the day's barometric pressure and temperature.

The farmer must know the current boiling temperature of water in order to boil the syrup to the correct density (sugar content). Finished syrup can also be

Maple syrup progressing through multiple pans in the evaporator

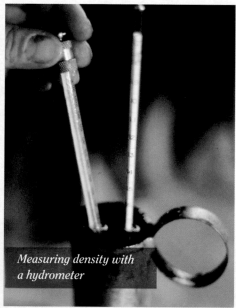

Measuring density with a hydrometer

determined by its density (about 11 pounds per gallon [1.32 kg/liter]) by examining the level at which a hydrometer floats in a sample. Some producers use a refracto-meter that measures the refractive index of a drop of the syrup, which is directly related to the amount of dissolved sugar in the solution.

FROM FINISH TO FILTER

Hot syrup from the finishing pan is filtered to remove what is called *niter*, or *sugar sand*, which is a naturally occurring precipitation of certain minerals in the sap. It can be puffy or sandy, and white to brown or black; the resultant amount is depen-dent — like all other aspects of syrup quality — on the age, health, and species of tree; the soil, climate, and weather; and even the time of day the sap was collected.

Two types of filters are commonly used: 1) a gravity system in which hot syrup is poured into a wool or Orlon felt bag and allowed to seep through; and 2) a pressure filter in which the syrup is pumped through a series of filter plates and disposable filter pads.

➤ HIGH-TECH TECHNIQUES ◄

Certain large-scale producers employ a few additional technologies for increasing their efficiencies and profit margins. In a process originally designed for desalinat-ing seawater, sap under pressure can be forced through a series of semiperme-able membranes with pores large enough for water molecules to pass through but not for those of sugar. This method, called *reverse osmosis*, can remove up to 75 percent of the water from sap before it is sent to the evaporator, thereby greatly reducing the time and fuel needed for the remainder of the processing.

A sap preheater, used to warm the temperature of the incoming sap, also reduces the amount of fuel required. Wood fuel can be burned more completely with the addition of a forced-draft blower to the firebox.

GIVING OUT GRADES

Syrup for wholesale or retail sale must meet national standards of minimum density and must be graded according to its flavor and percentage of light transmission. The individual bottler visually compares a sample of his syrup to a grading kit of glass standards or colored glycerin solutions.

For many years, the United States, Canada, and Vermont each had their own grading standards, which was a bit confusing at best. In 2015 Canada and the United States (including Vermont!) adopted a system of international standard definitions, grades and nomenclature for pure maple syrup. The new system clarifies that all pure maple syrup grades are processed in the same way and to the same level of purity and safety standards. Now it's all Grade A – with descriptors on color and taste:

- Grade A Golden Color, Delicate Taste
- Grade A Amber Color, Rich Taste
- Grade A Dark Color, Robust Taste
- Grade A Very Dark Color, Strong Taste

SYRUP GRADING STANDARDS

Sap sweetness and sugar concentration in syrup is measured in degrees Brix (°Brix), which is the food industry's accepted measurement for sweetness of fruit juices and other syrups. Standard minimum density for maple syrup is 66.0° Brix, meaning that 100 pounds of syrup contains 66.0 pounds of sugar.

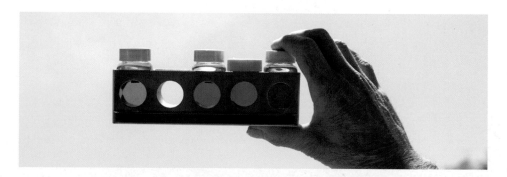

DIFFERENT NAMES, SAME STUFF

Former Grading Systems equivalents	International Maple Syrup Grading System
GRADE A LIGHT AMBER (USA) AND NO. 1 EXTRA LIGHT (CAN)	GRADE A GOLDEN COLOR, DELICATE TASTE
GRADE A MEDIUM AMBER (USA), NO. 1 LIGHT (CAN), GRADE A DARK AMBER (USA), AND NO. 1 MEDIUM	GRADE A AMBER COLOR, RICH TASTE
GRADE A DARK AMBER (USA), NO. 1 MEDIUM (CAN), GRADE B OR GRADE A EXTRA DARK (USA), AND NO. 2 AMBER (CAN)	GRADE A DARK COLOR, ROBUST TASTE
COMMERCIAL GRADE (USA) AND NO. 3 DARK (CAN)	GRADE A VERY DARK, COLOR STRONG TASTE

➤ TOP PRODUCERS ◄

Canada produces 83 percent of the world's supply of maple syrup. Its top provinces are:

#1 Quebec (world's largest supplier)
#2 Ontario
#3 New Brunswick
#4 Nova Scotia
#5 Prince Edward Island

In the United States, 16 states from Minnesota to Maine and south to West Virginia produce commercial syrup. While this ranking varies slightly from year to year, the U.S.'s top-producing states are:

#1 Vermont
#2 Maine
#3 New York
#4 Pennsylvania
#5 Ohio

OFF TO MARKET

To prevent contamination of filtered and finished syrup by mold or yeast growth, syrup is packaged while at least 180°F (82°C). The sealed cans or bottles are then inverted to expose the entire inside of the container and cap to the same sterilizing temperature. Syrup thus packaged will keep for many years with no problems; freezing extends that time considerably. Opened containers should be refrigerated. If crystals form, a tablespoon of water can be added and the syrup reheated to dissolve them.

MORE MAPLE PRODUCTS

By extending the processing of finished syrup, elevating its temperature to varying degrees above the boiling of water, and manipulating it in various ways, the well-diversified sugar maker can create and offer a variety of other popular maple products.

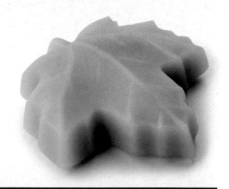

Product	Further method of processing
MAPLE SUGAR	STIRRED UNTIL CRYSTALLIZATION BEGINS, THEN POURED INTO MOLDS
GRANULATED MAPLE SUGAR	STIRRED UNTIL CRUMBLY, SIEVED THROUGH $\frac{5}{16}$" SCREEN
MAPLE CREAM (SPREAD, BUTTER)	RAPIDLY COOLED TO ROOM TEMPERATURE OR BELOW, THEN STIRRED TO CREAMY CONSISTENCY
MAPLE NOUGAT CANDY	COOLED AND DROPPED FREEFORM ON A MARBLE SLAB OR METAL SHEET OR PACKED INTO MOLDS
SOFT MOLDED SUGAR	STIRRED WHILE STILL HOT, THEN POURED OR PACKED INTO RUBBER MOLDS; POURING RESULTS IN A GLAZED SURFACE
SUGAR-ON-SNOW	POURED IMMEDIATELY WITHOUT STIRRING ONTO SNOW OR ICE, FORMING A THIN AND GLASSY TAFFY
ROCK CANDY	STORED AT ROOM TEMPERATURE FOR A LONG TIME; GROWS WELL-DEFINED SUCROSE CRYSTALS
MAPLE SNOW CONES	DARK AMBER SYRUP MIXED IN A CUPFUL OF GROUND ICE

THE MAPLE TREE
A CANADIAN SONG

BY SUSANNA MOODIE (1803–1885), CANADIAN POET, NOVELIST, AND ESSAYIST

When the snows of winter are melting fast,
And the sap begins to rise,
And the biting breath of the frozen blast
Yields to the Spring's soft sighs,
Then away to the wood,
For the maple, good,
Shall unlock its honied store;

And boys and girls,
With their sunny curls,
Bring their vessels brimming o'er
With the luscious flood
Of the brave tree's blood,
Into cauldrons deep to pour.

The blaze from the sugar-bush gleams red;
Far down in the forest dark,
A ruddy glow on the tree is shed,
That lights up the rugged bark;
And with merry shout,
The busy rout

Watch the sap as it bubbles high;
And they talk of the cheer
Of the coming year,
And the jest and the song pass by;
And brave tales of old
Round the fire are told,
That kindle youth's beaming eye.

Between 1876 and 1901, the maple leaf was on every Canadian coin, but today it remains on only the penny. In the United States, maple sugaring is featured on the Vermont quarter.

6

DO-IT-
YOURSELF

**Y**ou don't need to live in Vermont, talk like a Canadian, or own a thousand lidded buckets to make maple syrup (but then, it doesn't hurt, either!). Most any nearby live maple tree will yield enough sap for you to make at least a pint of syrup to enjoy with a meal of pancakes or waffles.

HOW TO TELL IF A TREE CAN BE TAPPED

Any native maple tree with a trunk diameter greater than 11 inches (28 cm) can be tapped (see chart below). Wherever the tree suffers from such stresses as wounds, disease, insects, soil compaction, pollution, or drought, it is better to go a little easier on it by placing fewer taps. Trees with large crowns extending down toward the ground are usually better sap producers. Follow the guidelines below for how many taps you can put in a tree.

Trunk diameter
(measured at 4½ feet (1.5 m) above the ground)

11–17 INCHES	1 TAP
18–24 INCHES	2 TAPS
24 INCHES AND UP	3 TAPS

While tapholes located on the south side of the tree may flow earlier than those on the north, east, or west (due to the sun's warming), there's no evidence that they yield more over the entire run than those on other sides of the tree. Likewise, locating a tap over a large root or below a large branch doesn't have an appreciable effect.

For ease of collecting, most taps are made between two and four feet (0.6–1.2 m) above the ground. You'll want to avoid any previous tapholes by five to six inches (13–15 cm) vertically and two to three inches (5–7.6 cm) from side to side, locating new tapholes slightly above or below them to keep wounds to a minimum. Using a bit size of five sixteenths (instead of the traditional seven sixteenths) creates smaller tapholes (promoted as *health spouts*) that heal faster and allow for more tappable area in future years.

TIMING THE TAPPING

Keep a close weather watch. The largest and most consistent sap flows begin when the daily maximum air temperature reaches into the upper 40s or low 50s (Fahrenheit; 7–12°C), while overnight lows still dip into the 20s (–6.6°C). Such a daily range forces the sap to rise from the roots and trunk toward the twigs to fuel the coming springtime growth spurt, which can happen anytime between February and April. Each tap on a healthy tree may produce 10 gallons of sap or more during the month-long season, with most of it coming during a 10- to 14-day "run," depending on the weather. Ten gallons of sap will yield about one quart of syrup.

The sugaring season ends as the buds on the twigs begin to pop open, the tree stops producing sugar, and the clear sap becomes cloudy and stops flowing.

The rate of flow of sap at its peak can equal 200 drops per minute or "two drops per heartbeat," as old sugarmakers say.

YOU CAN'T TAP TOO MUCH

A scar forms on the bark, but if the tree is otherwise healthy, tapping does not adversely affect the tree. If you follow the guidelines for the number of allowable taps per individual tree, no more than 10 percent of the tree's sap will be collected. This can be likened to your donating a pint of blood; you don't really miss it and your body simply produces more to replace what was taken. Some maples have been tapped upward of 150 years and are still healthy producers.

The word *spile* comes from the Dutch word for "splinter" or "peg."

Antique and contemporary spiles

STUFF YOU NEED TO MAKE SYRUP

To get started maple sugaring, you could spend a lot of money to purchase an elaborate system, but it can be done quite simply and frugally. A few supplies are all you need.

+ **Drill** with a sharp 5/16-inch bit
+ **Spiles** (collecting spouts) for the tapholes
+ **Collecting containers** (Plastic buckets and gallon milk jugs work just fine. If you use a bucket, a lid over it will help keep out twigs, debris, insects, snow, and rain.)
+ **Large shallow metal pan** or kettle
+ **Heat source** for boiling the sap (If you're using a wood fire, you'll need a sufficient stock of fuel and a stabilized grill on which to set your pan. A pair of cinder blocks with two or three metal yard stakes laid on top works well for this purpose. An outdoor grill or camp stove could also be pressed into service.)
+ **Candy thermometer** *optional* (One that registers at least 230°F [110°C] can help you keep track of the sap's progress and prevent burning of the syrup. Patience and a careful watch during finishing can do the same. Candy thermometers are readily available in houseware or kitchen departments.)
+ **Kitchen strainer** and paper towels or a sheet of white felt for filtering the finished syrup
+ **Storage containers** for the finished syrup

➤ FINDING THE EQUIPMENT ◄

Metal spiles with hooks, 500-foot (152 m) coils of plastic tubing and plastic spiles, as well as other sorts of professional equipment are available from any of the commercial suppliers listed in the Resources. Wooden spiles can be fashioned out of staghorn sumac stems by hollowing out the soft pith in the center of a piece 4 to 8 inches (10 to 20 cm) long. Even simple twigs can be fitted into the holes to allow the sap to drip away from the trunk.

LET'S GET TAPPING!

1   Identify the maples you intend to tap; gather your tools and equipment.

2   Locate the tap sites, using the chart on page 98 to determine the correct number for each tree.

3   Drill each hole 2 to 3 inches (5 to 8 cm) deep, slanting slightly upward into the trunk. Clear away any sawdust.

4   Insert the spile and tap it to a snug fit. (Don't pound it in!)

5   If using tubing, attach one end to the spile, set your bucket or jug on a stable spot on the ground, and let the other end of the tubing run down into it. If you are not using tubing, hang your bucket on the spile or tie it around the tree, or set it right below so the sap will drip directly into it.

6   Empty your container at least once every day, and more often if it is warm. Keep a close watch, because on a warm day the sap could overfill your jug and be wasted. Sap can spoil if left uncollected; if you want to save it to boil all at once, refrigerate it.

Running tubing into a milk jug

HOW LONG WILL THIS TAKE?

You are probably asking yourself questions such as: How long will it take to boil 40 gallons of sap? and How much firewood will I need? These questions beg other questions: How hot and how consistent will your heat source be? What is your elevation above sea level? What's the surface area and capacity of your pan? How many gallons are you starting with? What is the sugar content of your sap? What species of firewood are you burning? And other such concerns.

Here, for what it's worth, is the Herd Rule of Estimating Work Length (which is adaptable to nearly any task):

1. Estimate how long you *think* the job will take.
2. Add some more time to that.
3. Now double it.
4. Sigh.
5. Get started already.

SUGARING OFF

When you are ready to boil the sap, place it in a large shallow pan and heat it to a full, rolling boil. This is best done outside over an open fire if you have a lot of sap. (Check with your town fire department about this.)

Evaporating more than 10 gallons inside your home could peel the wallpaper off your walls! If you have only a few gallons to boil, however, putting a pot on the stove is convenient and easy. A dehumidifier and/or vent fan is still a good idea.

Boiling sap over an outdoor fire

As the sap evaporates, continue to add the remaining raw sap as room becomes available in the pan, but do not overfill, as it can boil over. The temperature of evaporating sap rises quite slowly at first, especially if you're continually adding new sap, but as the concentration of sugar increases, correspondingly less water is present to boil away, which means it can quite quickly boil over and burn. Keep an eye on it!

Touching the surface of the boiling sap with a stick of butter or adding an eighth of a teaspoon of cream prevents boiling over. You can rub some butter or vegetable oil on the rim of the pan for the same effect.

Only small quantities of sap should be boiled on a home stove.

The sap will eventually darken in color and thicken. The boiling liquid will be foamy, and as the water boils off and the sugar content increases, the bubbles reduce in size.

Finished sap boils at about 7°F above the boiling temperature of water (approximately 103.8°C), and as it nears this point, keep a careful watch on the pan to prevent burning the syrup. (As mentioned earlier, at higher elevations water's natural boiling point is less than 212°F (100°C): one degree Fahrenheit less for each 550 feet (168 m) of elevation above sea level. The day's temperature and barometric pressure also have an effect.)

As the syrup thickens, check its viscosity with a ladle or spoon. Runny, unfinished syrup simply drips off the spoon. When it aprons or sheets off the spoon in a single layer, it's done, though this method isn't always the most accurate, especially for a beginner. It's best to use a candy thermometer.

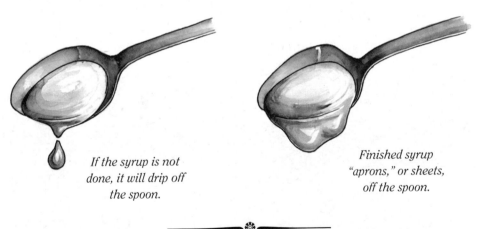

If the syrup is not done, it will drip off the spoon.

Finished syrup "aprons," or sheets, off the spoon.

You can quickly reduce the heat of a fire by raking coals away from the evaporator pan, or by shoveling snow on the fire. This is much easier and safer than trying to move or pick up a large, hot shallow pan without spilling your precious harvest and burning yourself in the process.

PACKAGING YOUR PRODUCT

While the syrup is still hot, filter it through a piece of clean felt, wool, cheesecloth, or even a couple layers of paper towels to remove the niter before you bottle it. If you skip this step, the sediment will settle on the bottom of the container and can make your syrup cloudy.

After filtering, can or bottle your syrup while it is still hot. Use a funnel to fill each sterilized lidded container almost to the brim so that very little air remains inside. Cap tightly and lay the containers sideways while they cool to create a better seal, and then store in a cool place. After opening, refrigerate.

Filtering hot syrup

If you don't have filter material, simply pour the syrup into an open container to sit for a few days. The sediment will settle to the bottom and then you can carefully pour or ladle off the clear syrup. Reheat it to almost boiling (180–185°F [82–85°C]) before pouring it into the containers for final storage.

If any harmless mold develops on the top of a batch of syrup that's been stored for several months, simply skim off the mold, reboil the syrup, and repackage into a sterile container.

CLEANUP IS CRITICAL

Clean out your pans, buckets, and filters by scrubbing with brushes or rags and hot water only, or with 1 part bleach to 20 parts water and double rinse. Do not use detergents because they can leave a film that can contaminate the flavor of future batches. Store your equipment in a dry place and keep covered until next year, when the sap run will once again beckon. Don't use your buckets and containers for any nonfood purposes.

SUGAR-ON-SNOW
A CLASSIC CONFECTION

Before you bottle up all that hard-won syrup, pour some of it directly onto a bowl full of clean snow or ice shavings. It will stiffen into a delectable taffy-like confection that can be picked up with forks or fingers and enjoyed immediately.

This treat has been part of the sugaring-off process for hundreds of years and is described in many accounts of pioneer life. Traditional accompaniments include donuts, with dill pickles to cut the sweetness.

2009 was a banner year for Canadian maple syrup production. The 109.4 million pounds of syrup collected that year eclipsed the previous record of 86.5 million pounds, set in 2004.

MAPLE
DELIGHTS

When you think about it, the healthful benefits of maple syrup are obvious: just look how tall and strong maple trees grow and how long they live. Not only is the wonderful elixir incredibly tasty but it is also nutritious, organic, versatile, and derived from a sustainable, native crop (which also happens to be among the handsomest of all trees).

One certainly cannot appreciate the lore, romance, and results of converting raw tree sap into an unparalleled delicacy without imbibing the final product. Imagine the honeybee not partaking of its life-work: It's unthinkable! Applied to fresh snow, ice cream, waffles, pancakes, oatmeal, applesauce, corn fritters, schnitzengruben — or anything else you care to try — maple syrup is the supreme treat topper. But its savory benevolence doesn't stop there!

GOOD AND GOOD FOR YOU

Maple syrup is a pure, all-natural sweetener, and other than honey and agave nectar, the only one in a naturally liquid state. It has no fat, no animal products, no artificial colors, and no preservatives. Unlike white cane sugar, which is stripped of its nutrients in its "refinement," or brown sugar, which is simply white sugar mixed with molasses, maple syrup is packed with vitamins, minerals, amino acids, and antioxidants. A little daily dose is like downing a good-tasting multivitamin pill.

Vitamins in maple syrup include niacin (B_3 or PP), pantothenic acid (B_5), riboflavin (B_2), and traces of folic acid, pyridoxine (B_6), biotin, and vitamin A. Minerals in the brew include potassium, calcium, magnesium, manganese, sodium, phosphorus, iron, zinc, copper, and tin. These levels are 15 times higher than those found in honey.

The carbohydrate composition of maple syrup is generally 88 to 99 percent sucrose, 0 to 11 percent hexoses (fructose and glucose), and trace amounts of other sugars. One ounce of maple syrup has 80 calories (the same as molasses), compared with 90 for honey and 120 for corn syrup.

A quarter-cup serving contains 100 percent of the recommended daily allowance of manganese, 34 percent of riboflavin, and 11 percent of zinc.

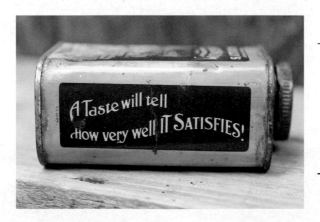

A Taste will tell how very well IT SATISFIES!

A one-ounce serving of maple syrup has 73 calories. A serving of honey has 85.

COOKING AND BAKING WITH MAPLE

As a versatile ingredient in breads, desserts, snacks, beverages, vegetables, and meat dishes, as well as sauces, glazes, and marinades, maple syrup adds depth and intriguing complexity to the pleasure of the palate and contributes to the joy of zesty cooking. It easily substitutes for honey, molasses, and corn syrup in recipes on an equal basis and can be substituted for white sugar with minor adjustments.

According to the good folks at Michigan State University Cooperative Extension Service, you can substitute one and a half cups of pure maple syrup for each cup of granulated sugar and add one quarter teaspoon baking soda for each cup of maple syrup used. When maple syrup is substituted for all the sugar in a recipe, reduce the amount of liquid used by one-half. If maple syrup is substituted for half the sugar, reduce liquid amounts by one-fourth.

CERTIFIED MAPLE SYRUPS

By definition, organic means that the food has no artificial preservatives and that the trees have had no contact with pesticides or fertilizers for a proscribed amount of time. However, to be Certified Organic Maple Syrup (which should be stated on the label), three criteria must be followed:

- ✦ No chemicals may be used to manage the sugar bush.
- ✦ Farmers adhere to a standard to limit the number of taps per tree.
- ✦ Inspectors confirm the cleanliness of all the processing equipment.

To be certified kosher, the production process must conform to Jewish food-making standards. Kosher syrup producers are inspected every one to two weeks by a rabbi.

GOING BY GRADE

Grade A, No. 1, or Fancy maple syrup, made from sap harvested early in the season, is generally clearer and lighter in taste, and is a favorite among breakfast gourmets. As the season progresses, the syrup darkens in color and becomes more caramelized. Grade B, or Amber, syrup, with its more robust flavor, is usually the choice of cooks and chefs for enhancing other dishes.

Canada's No. 3 Dark and Vermont's Commercial grades are most often destined for use in large-batch commercial products, such as flavoring confections, granolas, cereals, pudding, ice cream, and — believe it or not — tobacco.

IT'S NOT JUST FOR PANCAKES

For everyone who has appreciative taste buds, here's the opportunity to indulge your sweet yearnings in bringing your liquid harvest to the hearth; a broad range of maple syrup recipes, collected from a variety of sources, can be found on the following pages. But if you're like me in the kitchen (and let's truly hope you're not — my wife keeps booting me out of ours), the only recipes you dare attempt are the foolproof ones. Provided you know where the pans are kept and how to turn on the oven, most of these recipes are simple enough that even I, the guy who once unthinkingly fried popcorn kernels in an uncovered pan, can do them.

So, go ahead and cultivate your culinary cravings. Here's to pleasing the palate with the pure, sweet, matchless gift of the maple! Bon appétit!

Maple Fudge, page 131

MAPLE NUT BREAD

1 cup walnuts, chopped
½ cup maple syrup
3 cups commercial
    baking mix
½ cup sugar
1 egg
1¼ cups milk

1. Several hours before making bread, mix walnuts and maple syrup and let stand. This step can also be done two or three days ahead and refrigerated.

2. Preheat oven to 350°F (175°C). Grease a 9- by 5- by 3-inch loaf pan.

3. Mix baking mix, sugar, egg, and milk in a large bowl. Beat well for 30 seconds.

4. Stir in walnut mixture.

5. Pour the batter into the prepared pan. Bake 45 to 50 minutes until toothpick inserted into center comes out clean. Cool before slicing.

YIELD: 1 LOAF

MAPLE WALNUT MUFFINS

2 cups flour

2 tablespoons sugar

1 tablespoon baking powder

½ teaspoon salt

4 tablespoons (½ stick) butter, softened

1 egg

¾ cup maple syrup

¼ cup milk

½ cup walnuts, chopped

1. Preheat oven to 400°F (205°C). Grease muffin tins.

2. Combine flour, sugar, baking powder, and salt in a large bowl. Add softened butter and mix well.

3. Add egg, syrup, and milk, stirring until well blended. Fold in walnuts.

4. Fill muffin tins a little more than half-full with batter. Bake for 20 to 25 minutes.

YIELD: 12 MUFFINS

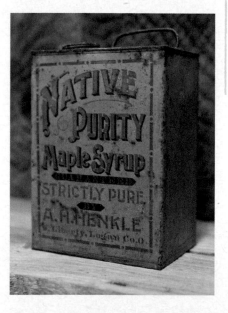

MAPLE SUGAR BISCUITS

2 cups flour
4 teaspoons baking powder
½ teaspoon salt
¼ cup vegetable shortening
1 cup maple syrup
¾ cup milk
4 tablespoons (½ stick) butter, softened
3–4 tablespoons maple sugar
2–3 teaspoons cinnamon

1. Preheat oven to 400°F (205°C). Grease a baking sheet.

2. Sift the flour, baking powder, and salt into a bowl.

3. Cut in the shortening until the mixture is pea-sized.

4. Add milk and syrup to make a soft dough.

5. Pat or roll out dough to a thickness of ½ inch, and cut with small biscuit cutter.

6. Place on baking sheet.

7. Spread with softened butter and sprinkle with maple sugar and cinnamon.

8. Bake for about 15 minutes until lightly browned.

YIELD: ABOUT 16 BISCUITS

MAPLE MILKSHAKE

2 cups milk
1 cup light cream or half-
and-half
½ cup maple syrup
2 scoops favorite ice cream

Mix the milk, cream, maple syrup, and ice cream in a blender until frothy, and serve.

YIELD: 2 SERVINGS

MAPLE FIZZ

1 quart milk
¼ cup maple syrup
12 ounces ginger ale

1. Mix milk and maple syrup in a blender.

2. Pour into tall glasses to about two-thirds full.

3. Top off with ginger ale.

YIELD: 6 SERVINGS

MAPLE EGG NOG

6 eggs
¾ cup sugar
2 quarts milk
1 cup maple syrup
1 teaspoon vanilla
½ teaspoon salt
Whipped cream
Pinch of nutmeg

NOTE: This recipe calls for using raw egg yolks. You can use pasteurized eggs here. If you opt not to, do not serve this recipe to those for whom the consumption of raw eggs poses a serious health risk, including children under the age of four, the elderly, pregnant women, and anyone with a compromised immune system.

1. Separate egg yolks from egg whites.

2. In a large bowl, use an electric mixer to beat ¼ cup of the sugar and the egg yolks until the mixture is thick and pale yellow.

3. With clean beaters, beat egg whites in a separate bowl, gradually adding the remaining ½ cup sugar, until stiff.

4. Fold egg yolk mixture into egg whites.

5. Stir in milk, maple syrup, vanilla, and salt.

6. Chill and serve with a dollop of whipped cream and grated nutmeg sprinkled on top.

YIELD: 8 SERVINGS

HOT MAPLE APPLE CIDER

6 cups apple cider
¼ cup maple syrup
2 cinnamon sticks
6 whole cloves
6 whole allspice berries
1 orange peel, cut into strips
1 lemon peel, cut into strips
Spice bag and string
Additional cinnamon sticks, citrus slices, or whipped cream, optional

1. Pour cider and syrup into large pot.

2. Place spices and citrus peels in a spice bag and tie up with a piece of string.

3. Drop spice bundle into the cider mixture.

4. Heat over moderate heat for about 10 minutes.

5. Remove spice bag and discard.

6. Ladle maple cider into mugs and serve warm.

If desired, garnish with additional sticks of cinnamon for stirring, thin slices of lemon or orange, or whipped cream.

YIELD: 6–8 SERVINGS

MAPLE AND BALSAMIC VINEGAR DRESSING

3 tablespoons balsamic vinegar
2 tablespoons maple syrup
1 tablespoon lime juice
1 teaspoon dry mustard
1 teaspoon fresh cilantro, chopped
1 clove garlic, minced
1 cup extra-virgin olive oil
½ teaspoon salt
¼ teaspoon freshly ground black pepper

1. Mix together the vinegar, syrup, lime juice, mustard, cilantro, and garlic.

2. Add olive oil in a slow stream, whisking constantly until dressing is emulsified.

3. Season with salt and pepper to taste.

Store in refrigerator; will keep for several weeks.

YIELD: ABOUT 1¼ CUPS

MAPLE CHERRY SAUCE

⅓ cup cherry juice

2 tablespoons cornstarch

1 cup frozen tart or sweet
  cherries, thawed and
  well drained

¾ cup maple syrup

½ cup walnuts, chopped

1 teaspoon orange zest

NOTE: 1 (16-ounce) can tart cherries or sweet cherries, well drained, can be substituted for frozen tart or sweet cherries.

1. Mix thoroughly the cherry juice and cornstarch in a small saucepan.

2. Cook over medium heat until thickened.

3. Stir in cherries, maple syrup, walnuts, and orange zest.

4. Cook over low heat, stirring frequently, until all ingredients are hot.

Serve warm; excellent with roast pork, ham, or turkey.

MAKES 1½ CUPS

BAKED BEANS

4 cups cooked beans (dried
  lima, navy, or beans of
  your preference), or 2
  (15-ounce) cans, rinsed
  and drained
1 cup maple syrup
1 teaspoon salt
¼ teaspoon dry mustard
⅛ teaspoon freshly ground
  black pepper
¼ pound sliced bacon

1. Preheat oven to 300°F (150°C).

2. Combine beans, syrup, salt, mustard, and
   pepper in a casserole dish.

3. Lay bacon slices across the top of the
   mixture.

4. Bake uncovered for 4 hours.

YIELD: 6–8 SERVINGS

MAPLE PECAN PEAS

½ cup maple syrup
¼ cup pecans, coarsely
  chopped
1 (10-ounce) package
  frozen peas

1. Heat syrup and pecans in a small saucepan over medium heat for 5 minutes.

2. Stir in frozen peas and heat until peas
   are hot.

YIELD: 4 SERVINGS

MAPLE NUTMEG BUTTERNUT SQUASH

1 butternut squash
(1½ pounds)
3 tablespoons butter, softened
1 tablespoon maple syrup
¾ teaspoon salt
¼ teaspoon nutmeg

1. Peel and dice squash, discarding seeds.

2. Cook in a small amount of salted boiling water until tender, then drain.

3. Place squash in a bowl and beat until smooth.

4. Add butter, maple syrup, salt, and nutmeg, stirring well.

5. Sprinkle with additional nutmeg before serving.

YIELD: ABOUT 6 SERVINGS

MAPLE-GLAZED HAM

1 ham, size of your
     choosing
Handful of whole cloves
¼–½ cup maple syrup
Sprinkling of maple sugar,
     optional

1. Preheat oven to 350°F (175°C).

2. Skin and score ham; place in baking pan.

3. Stick surface of ham with whole cloves.

4. Bake for appropriate length of time
   for the given size ham. Approximately
   halfway through baking, drizzle with
   maple syrup. Baste the ham with the
   drippings several times during the latter
   part of baking, or sprinkle with maple
   sugar.

SWEET AND SOUR CHICKEN

¾ cup juice from canned
  pineapple or ¾ cup
  pineapple juice
¼ cup maple syrup
2 tablespoons cornstarch
½ teaspoon salt
¼ cup vinegar
1 tablespoon soy sauce
3 cups chicken, cooked and
  sliced
¼ cup onion, thinly sliced
1 cup canned pineapple
  chunks (packed in
  juice), drained
½ cup celery, sliced in thin
  strips, 1 inch in length
½ cup green pepper, chopped
2 tablespoons pimento,
  diced
2 (3-ounce) cans chow
  mein noodles, or 2 cups
  cooked rice
¼ cup almonds, toasted and
  slivered

1. Pour pineapple liquid into saucepan.

2. Combine maple syrup, cornstarch, and salt, and pour into the pineapple liquid.

3. Add vinegar and soy sauce.

4. Bring to a boil over high heat. Reduce heat and cook until thick, stirring constantly.

5. Add onion, pineapple, celery, and green pepper, and cook for 5 minutes.

6. Add chicken and cook for 5 more minutes.

7. Add pimento and cook for another minute.

8. Ladle over noodles or rice. Garnish with almonds before serving.

YIELD: SERVES 6

PORK CHOPS WITH MAPLE BARBECUE SAUCE

FOR THE SAUCE

¼ cup onion, minced

1 can condensed tomato
   soup

¼ cup maple syrup

¼ cup vinegar

1 tablespoon
   Worcestershire sauce

1 tablespoon soy sauce

1 teaspoon dry mustard

4 pork chops

1. Preheat broiler. Position the oven rack in the second from the top slot.

2. Combine sauce ingredients in a small pan over medium-low heat.

3. Heat until sauce is warm and blended.

4. Broil pork chops for about 8 minutes, then flip and broil for 8 minutes longer. Turn chops again, baste with sauce and broil for 2 minutes. Flip them once more, baste with sauce, and broil for 2 minutes. This process can be smoky, so turn on your vent fan or open a window.

   You can also prepare these pork chops outside on a grill. Use an instant-read thermometer to make sure the meat has reached an internal temperature of 155°F (68°C) before serving.

YIELD: 4 SERVINGS

MAPLE-GLAZED SALMON

FOR THE GLAZE

  2 tablespoons maple syrup

1½ tablespoons apple juice

1½ tablespoons fresh lemon
     juice

  2 teaspoons hoisin sauce

1½ peeled and grated
     teaspoons, fresh ginger

1½ teaspoons Dijon mustard

¼ teaspoon five-spice
     powder

  4 (6-ounce) salmon fillets
     (about 1 inch thick)

Cooking spray

1. Combine ingredients for the glaze in a large ziplock plastic bag or lidded container large enough to hold the fish.

2. Add salmon to the bag or container; seal. Marinate in refrigerator for 15 minutes.

3. Preheat broiler while salmon is marinating.

4. Remove salmon from the bag, reserving marinade. Place salmon fillets, skin side down, on a broiler rack coated with cooking spray.

5. Basting salmon occasionally with the reserved marinade, broil for 12 minutes or until the fish flakes easily when tested with a fork.

YIELD: 4 SERVINGS

— adapted from a recipe in *Cooking Light Magazine*

DELUXE PECAN PIE

3 eggs

1 cup sugar

2 tablespoons butter, melted

¾ cup light or dark corn syrup

¼ cup maple syrup

1 teaspoon vanilla

⅛ teaspoon salt

1 cup pecans or walnuts, coarsely chopped

9-inch unbaked pastry shell

1. Preheat oven to 350°F (175°C).

2. Beat eggs slightly in medium bowl with a mixer at medium speed.

3. Add sugar, butter, corn syrup, maple syrup, vanilla, and salt and mix well.

4. Stir in nuts.

5. Pour into pastry shell.

6. Bake for 55 to 60 minutes or until knife inserted halfway between center and edge comes out clean. Cool before slicing.

YIELD: ONE 9-INCH PIE

MAPLE SPONGE CAKE

4 eggs
¾ cup maple syrup
½ teaspoon vanilla
1 cup sifted cake flour
½ teaspoon baking powder
¼ teaspoon salt

1. Preheat oven to 325°F (165°C).

2. Separate egg whites from egg yolks. In a large bowl, beat egg whites until stiff but not dry. Set aside.

3. In a small bowl, beat yolks until light and fluffy. Fold the syrup, vanilla, flour, baking powder, and salt into egg yolks. Gently fold yolk mixture into egg whites.

4. Pour batter into a greased, lightly floured 10-inch tube pan and bake for 50 minutes.

YIELD: 1 CAKE

MAPLE FUDGE

2 egg whites
3 cups maple syrup
⅔ cup light corn syrup
1 teaspoon baking powder
1 cup walnut pieces

1. Beat egg whites to stiff peaks and set aside.

2. Stir maple syrup and corn syrup together in a small saucepan over medium to high heat, stirring constantly with a wooden spoon; boil until a drop forms a hard ball in cold water (250°–260°F [121°–126°C] on a candy thermometer).

3. Pour syrup mixture in a slow stream over stiffly beaten egg whites, beating constantly. Cool to 110°F (43°C).

4. For the last of the cooling, use a large spoon to beat the fudge until it begins to set. When stiff in texture, stir in baking powder and walnuts.

5. Pour into a greased 8 × 8 pan. Cut the firm, cooled fudge into squares.

MAPLE MOUSSE

2 egg yolks

½ cup maple syrup

⅛ teaspoon salt

½ pint heavy cream, whipped

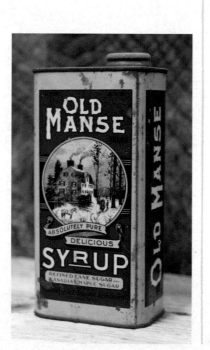

1. Bring 1 inch of water to a boil in the bottom of a double boiler.

2. Beat yolks in the top of the double boiler (off the heat) until they turn a lemon color.

3. Heat maple syrup and salt to boiling in a small saucepan, then pour slowly into the egg yolks, whisking continuously. Cook gently over simmering water on low heat until the egg mixture coats a spoon. Cool to room temperature, stirring frequently.

4. Fold whipped cream into egg yolk mixture, pour into serving dishes, and chill.

YIELD: 4 SERVINGS

MAPLE CANDY APPLES

¼ teaspoon butter, if needed
2 cups maple syrup
6 medium apples

1. In a small saucepan over high heat, boil syrup to 236°F (113°C).

2. Add butter to prevent foaming, if needed.

3. Set pan in cold water until syrup cools to 150°F (65°C).

4. Beat until syrup turns creamy.

5. Spear each apple with a popsicle stick, coat apple with whipped syrup, and let cool.

YIELD: 6 APPLES

POPCORN BALLS

1½ cups maple syrup
⅛ teaspoon cream of tartar
1 tablespoon butter
8 cups popped corn

1. In a small saucepan over high heat, boil syrup and cream of tartar to hard ball stage (meaning it forms a firm round blob when a drop lands in a bowl of cold water) or until it reaches 265°F [130°C] on a candy thermometer.

2. Remove from heat, stir in butter, and pour mixture over the popcorn.

3. Shape into balls while warm. Avoid a sticky mess by either buttering your hands or dipping them in cold water before you begin handling the popcorn.

YIELD: 10 BALLS

MAPLE GRANOLA

4 cups old-fashioned rolled oats

1 cup each coarsely chopped walnuts and unsalted peanuts

1 cup hulled sunflower seeds

6 tablespoons maple syrup

6 tablespoons vegetable or canola oil

1 cup raisins and chopped dates, combined

1. Preheat oven to 300°F (150°C).

2. Mix oats, nuts, and seeds in a large bowl.

3. Combine syrup & oil in a small bowl and microwave 30 seconds until warm. Pour over dry oat mixture.

4. Work the combined ingredients with your hands until material is uniformly moist, then spread on a lightly greased or nonstick cookie sheet.

5. Bake for 30 minutes, stirring occasionally, until golden in color.

6. Cool granola to room temperature and stir in dried fruit. Store in well-sealed jars or plastic bags.

YIELD: ABOUT 8 CUPS

MAPLE CREAM

2 cups maple syrup
Vegetable oil or butter

1. Cook syrup, without stirring, on medium-high heat in a large, heavy pot until it reaches 235°F (113°C). Add a few drops of oil or a tiny bit of butter to keep it from foaming.

2. Remove from heat and set pan into a sink of cold water making sure no water gets into the syrup. Cool syrup rapidly to approximately 125°F (51.6°C); do not stir while cooling.

3. Beat with an electric mixer until creamy and light-colored. Do not cool too long or overbeat or the mixture will harden.

4. Spoon into a glass or plastic container with a lid. Keep refrigerated.

Spread on toast or muffins, use in a peanut butter sandwich instead of jelly, drop some on fruit salad, whatever you can think of!

YIELD: 1 CUP

APPENDIX

𓃰𓃰𓃰𓃰𓃰𓃰𓃰𓃰𓃰𓃰𓃰𓃰𓃰𓃰𓃰𓃰𓃰𓃰𓃰𓃰

MAPLE FESTIVALS

Witness first-hand — or even lend a hand to — the tapping/collecting/boiling/sugaring-off process, and taste the sweet results of hard work done well. Immerse yourself in all things maple with a visit to a Maple Festival near you!

Found throughout the syrup-producing country, with most held annually on the same weekends each year, many Maple Festivals offer much more than a mere visit to the sugar bush (though that's always reason enough!) with a slew of additional homegrown attractions.

Enjoy all-you-can-eat, syrup-drenched pancake breakfasts, syrup- and candy-making demonstrations, arts and crafts shows, musical entertainment, tractor pulls, dancing, parades, horse-drawn sleighs, hayrides, antiques shows, museum and nature center tours, and much more!

CANADA

BRITISH COLUMBIA

Bigleaf Maple Syrup Festival
   BC Forest Discovery Centre
   Duncan, British Columbia
   250-715-1113
   www.bcforestdiscoverycentre.com

Maple Sugar Festival du Sucre d'Érable
   Nanaimo, British Columbia
   250-729-2776
   www.art-bc.com

NOVA SCOTIA

Maple Producers' Association of Nova Scotia
   www.novascotiamaplesyrup.com
   The MPANS hosts multiple festivals throughout Nova Scotia.

ONTARIO

Elmira Maple Syrup Festival
   Elmira, Ontario
   877-969-0094
   www.elmiramaplesyrup.com

Elmvale Maple Syrup Festival
   Elmvale, Ontario
   705-322-6613
   www.elmvalemaplesyrup.ca

Festival of Maples
   The Perth & District Chamber of Commerce
   Perth, Ontario
   888-319-3204
   www.beautifulperth.com/maples.html

Holstein Maplefest
Holstein, Ontario
519-334-3490
www.holsteinmaplefest.com

Maple Syrup Festival
Friends of Killbear Park
Nobel, Ontario
705-342-5492
www.friendsofkillbear.com

Maple in the County
Bloomfield, Ontario
www.mapleinthecounty.ca

Buckhorn Maplefest
McLean Berry Farm
Buckhorn, Ontario
705-657-2134
www.mcleanberryfarm.com

Powassan Maple Syrup Festival
Powassan, Ontario
chair@powassansyrupfestival.ca
www.powassansyrupfestival.ca

Sunderland Maple Syrup Festival
Sunderland, Ontario
www.maplesyrupfestival.ca

Sugarbush Maple Syrup Festival
Woodbridge and Stouffville, Ontario
416-667-6299
http://maplesyrupfest.com

Warkworth Maple Syrup Festival
Warkworth, Ontario
705-924-2057
www.warkworthmaplesyrupfestival.ca

QUEBEC

Festival Beauceron de l'Erable
Saint-Georges, Quebec
418-228-4983
www.festivalbeaucerondelerable.com

UNITED STATES
CONNECTICUT
Hebron Maple Festival
Hebron, Connecticut
info@hebronmaplefest.com
www.hebronmaplefest.com

ILLINOIS
Illinois Maple Syrup Festivals and Producers
www.enjoyillinois.com

INDIANA
*Leane and Michael's Sugarbush Annual
   Maple Syrup Festival*
Salem, Indiana
www.lmsugarbush.com/ourfestival.html

National Maple Syrup Festival
Medora, Indiana
www.nationalmaplesyrupfestival.com

Parke County Maple Syrup Fair
Rockville, Indiana
765-569-5226
www.parkecounty.com

Wakarusa Maple Syrup Festival
Wakarusa, Indiana
574-862-4344
www.wakarusachamber.com/
maple-syrup-festival

MAINE
Maine Maple Syrup Festivals and Producers
www.mainstreetskowhegan.org

MARYLAND
Annual Maple Syrup Program
Cunningham Falls State Park
Thurmont, Maryland
301-271-7574
www.dnr.maryland.gov

MICHIGAN

Annual Maple Sugar Festival
Kalamazoo, Michigan
269-381-1574
www.naturecenter.org
Michigan Maple Syrup Festivals and Producers
www.mi-maplesyrup.com
Vermontville Maple Syrup Festival
Vermontville, Michigan
www.vermontvillemaplesyrupfestival.com

NEW YORK

Maple Weekend
Wyoming County Maple Producers
Association
585-591-1190
www.nysmaple.com

OHIO

Geauga County Maple Festival
Chardon, Ohio
440-286-3007
www.maplefestival.com
Ohio Maple Syrup Festivals and Producers
www.ohiomaple.org
Sugar Maple Festival
Bellbrook, Ohio
www.sugarmaplefestival.com

PENNSYLVANIA

Endless Mountains Maple Festival
Troy, Pennsylvania
570-297-3648
www.maplefestivalpa.com
Northwest Pennsylvania Maple Association
814-796-3699
www.pamaple.org
Pennsylvania Maple Festival
Meyersdale, Pennsylvania
814-634-0213
www.pamaplefestival.com

VERMONT

Vermont Maple Festival
St. Albans, Vermont
www.vtmaplefestival.org
Vermont Maple Syrup Festivals and Producers
www.vermontmaple.org

VIRGINIA

Highland Maple Festival
Highland County Chamber of Commerce
www.highlandcounty.org

WEST VIRGINIA

Maple Days
www.wvtourism.com/event/mapledays

RESOURCES

COLLECTING AND PROCESSING EQUIPMENT

Bascom's Maple Farms, Inc.
Alstead, New Hampshire
603-835-6361
www.bascommaple.com
Lapierre Equipment Inc
Beauce, Québec
819-548-5454
www.elapierre.com
Leader Evaporator Co.
Swanton, Vermont
802-868-5444
www.leaderevaporator.com
Sugar Bush Supply Co.
Mason, Michigan
517-349-5185
http://sugarbushsupplies.com

OTHER RESOURCES

For local and regional information on maple trees, syrup production, producers and equipment suppliers, contact your county's Agricultural Extension Service office; most have agents who can help with your request or can refer you to someone who can.

American Maple Museum
Croghan, New York
315-346-1107
www.maplemuseumcentre.org
Preserves the history and evolution of the North American maple syrup industry
New Hampshire Maple Museum
New Hampshire Maple Producers Association
Bethlehem, New Hampshire
603-225-3757
www.nhmapleproducers.com/museum.html
The North American Maple Syrup Producers Manual, 2nd ed. 2006.
A 180-page manual developed by the Ohio State University Extension in cooperation with The North American Maple Syrup Council. Available online at Ohio State University Extension's Publication online store (http://extensionpubs.osu.edu) or can be ordered in book form from many of the maple producers associations.

YouTube
www.youtube.com
Search for "maple syrup production" to view many interesting videos from the sugar bush.

PRODUCERS ASSOCIATIONS — CANADA

Maple Producers' Association of Nova Scotia
Springhill, Nova Scotia
902-597-2645
www.novascotiamaplesyrup.com
Maple Syrup Producers' Cooperative
Plessisville, Quebec
819-362-3241
www.citadelle-camp.coop
New Brunswick Maple Syrup Association Inc.
Fredericton, New Brunswick
506-458-8889
www.maplesyrupnb.com
Ontario Maple Syrup Producers Association
Bailieboro, Ontario
866-566-2753
www.ontariomaple.com

PRODUCERS ASSOCIATIONS — USA

Maple Syrup Producers Association of Connecticut
Windsor, Connecticut
info@ctmaple.org
www.ctmaple.org
Indiana Maple Syrup Association
Roanoke, Indiana
www.indianamaplesyrup.org
Maine Maple Producers Association
Newfield, Maine
www.mainemapleproducers.com
Massachusetts Maple Producers Association
Plainfield, Massachusetts
413-628-3912
www.massmaple.org
Michigan Maple Syrup Association
Bellevue, Michigan
www.mi-maplesyrup.com

New Hampshire Maple Producers Association
Warner, New Hampshire
603-225-3757
www.nhmapleproducers.com
New York State Maple Producers Association
Syracuse, New York
office@nysmaple.com
www.nysmaple.com
Ohio Maple Producers Association
Wooster, Ohio
www.ohiomapleproducers.com
Pennsylvania Maple Syrup Producers Council
Springville, Pennsylvania
www.pamapleassociation.com
Vermont Maple Sugar Makers' Association
South Royalton, Vermont
802-763-7435
www.vermontmaple.org
Wisconsin Maple Syrup Producers Association
Holcombe, Wisconsin
920-680-9320
www.wismaple.org

INTERNATIONAL ASSOCIATIONS
The International Maple Syrup Institute
Spencerville, Ontario
613-658-2329
www.internationalmaplesyrupinstitute.com
Promotes the use of pure maple syrup, protects the integrity of the product, and encourages cooperation among all involved in the maple industry.
North American Maple Syrup Council
Simsbury, Connecticut
www.northamericanmaple.org
An international network of maple syrup producer associations representing 16 commercial maple-producing states and provinces

INDEX

ACKNOWLEDGMENTS: This project started with the hundreds of times I presented educational programs on maple sugaring to school groups, scouts, families, and other late-winter park visitors, all seeking the sweet romance of the history, science, lore, and literal taste of the maple — and the trees' connection to their sense of place. Thanks for the interest and attention!

I am particularly grateful to my friend Liz Walker of Walker Publishing Services, who spent countless hours helping me "tap" more of this book's conceptual potential; to my agent, Deirdre Mullane, who helped me "collect and filter" more of the raw material and develop it for the market; and to my editor, Lisa Hiley, who, with the entire Storey Publishing team, "refined and packaged" the final delightful product.

Special thanks to Beverly Duncan for her excellent, engaging illustrations and to Tom McCrumm of South Face Farm, Ashfield, Massachusetts, who opened his amazing collection of vintage tins, tools, and utensils to us.

INTERIOR PHOTOGRAPHY CREDITS

© Nathan Benn/Alamy 86 top
© Roderick Chen/Getty Images 104, 108
© Will Cook 60 left
© Cornell University 88
© Louis DiBacco/iStockphoto 39
© Stephen G. Donaldson 63, 86 bottom
© Sabine Vollmer von Falken 27 right
© GAP Photos Ltd./Richard Bloom 58
© GAP Photos/Julie Dansereau 8
© GAP Photos/John Glover 11
© Getty Images 25
© Richard Gillard/iStockphoto 69
© Michael Grand/StockFood 93
© Stéphane Groleau/Alamy 34–35
© Robert S. Hansen 81
© Hemis/Alamy 87
© Wolfgang Hoffmann/AGStock USA 72
© INTERFOTO/Alamy 17
© Lonely Planet images/Alamy 85
© Sandy Macys/Alamy 66 right

© Patricia Toth McCormick/Getty Images 38
© National Geographic Image Collection/Alamy 27 left
© Nativestock.com/Marilyn Angel Wynn/Getty Images 16
© New England Pix/Alamy 33
© Jerry Pavia 59, 60 right
© Plainpicture/Glasshouse Images 6, 62, 66 left
© Paul Poplis Photography, Inc./StockFood 113, 114
© Philip Scala/Alamy 84
© Joanne Schmaltz/StockFood 110
© Lynn Stone 29, 64–65, 83, 92
© Superstock/Getty Images 36
© Teri Studios/StockFood 80
© Vespasian/Alamy 2
Mars Vilaubi 14, 15, 41, 90, 95, 98, 100, 106–107, 11, 116, 121, 124, 125, 131, 132–133, 134, 136
© Janusz Wrobel/Alamy 18, 28